The Shorter Revised
LATIN PRIMER

By

Benjamin Hall Kennedy, DD

Revised & Updated
Simon Wallenberg Press 2007

© 2007 Simon Wallenberg ISBN 1-84356-031-3
The Shorter Revised Latin Primer
Benjamin Hall Kennedy

This is an updated version of The Shorter Revised Latin
Primer With Chapters from the Public School Latin Primer
and Public School Latin Grammar has been rearranged,
revised and improved by the Simon Wallenburg Press.

The Shorter Revised Latin Primer - Eight Edition Published London 1908 -This Edition Revised Improved &
Enlarged by Simon Wallenberg Press 2007

An Wallenberg Grammar Book

Published by the Simon Wallenberg Press
wallenberg.press@gmail.com

Copyright revision: Simon Wallenberg
© Book Block & Cover design Wallenberg Press, Printed
in the United States of America & The United Kingdom.

Printed on acid-free paper.

Benjamin Hall Kennedy
(November 6, 1804 – April 6, 1880)

Was an English scholar. He was born at Summer Hill, near
Birmingham, the eldest son of Rann Kennedy (1772–1851),
of a branch of the Ayrshire family which had settled in Staf-
fordshire.

Rann was a scholar and man of letters, several of whose sons
rose to distinction. Benjamin was educated at Shrewsbury
School, and St John's College, Cambridge. After a brilliant
university career he was elected fellow and classical lecturer
of St John's College in 1828. Two years later he became an
assistant master at Harrow, whence he went to Shrewsbury
as headmaster in 1836. He retained this post until 1866, the
thirty years being marked by a long series of successes for
his pupils, chiefly in classics.

When he retired from Shrewsbury a large collection was
made, and was used partly on new school buildings and
partly on the founding of a Latin professorship at Cambridge. The first holders were both Kennedy's old pupils,
HAJ Munro and JEB Mayor. In 1867, Kennedy was elected
Regius Professor of Greek at Cambridge and canon of Ely
Cathedral.

From 1870 to 1880 he was a member of the committee for
the revision of the New Testament. He supported the admis-
sion of women to university, and took a prominent part in the
establishment of Newnham and Girton colleges.

In politics, he had liberal sympathies. Among a number of
classical school-books published by him are two, a Public
School Latin Primer and Public School Latin Grammar,

which were for long in use in nearly all English schools. He died near Torquay.

His other chief works are: Sophocles, Oedipus Tyrannus (2nd ed., 1885), Aristophanes, Birds (1874); Aeschylus, Agamemnon (2nd ed1882), with introduction, metrical translation and notes; a commentary on Virgil (3rd ed., 1881); and a translation of Plato, Theaetetus (1881).

He contributed largely to the collection known as Sabrinae Corolla, and published a collection of verse in Greek, Latin and English under the title of Between Whiles (2nd ed., 1882), with many autobiographical details.

Kennedy's Books remain popular right up to the present day for students of the Latin Language.

All of Benjamin hall Kennedy's language Books in their Revised and updated editions are published by the Simon Wallenberg Press.

PREFACE.

———◦•◦———

THIS little book is published in compliance with a wish expressed to me by a large number of Masters, including many teachers in Preparatory Schools, and in the lower forms of Public Schools.

It is intended to be a simple manual for beginners in Latin, preparatory to the use of the Revised Latin Primer.

In order to facilitate the passage of the learner from one book to the other, and also to make it possible for them to be used side by side if necessary, this Shorter Primer has been made, as far as it goes, in the main identical with the Revised Primer, and arranged on the same plan.

It contains the memorial portion of the Accidence, with a few of the most important notes and explanations, and the more elementary parts of the Syntax of the Simple Sentence.

A short outline of the Compound Sentence, which did not form part of my original plan, has been added in accordance with the desire of several experienced teachers. In this part it has been necessary, for the sake of brevity, to make the arrangement and wording somewhat different from that of the Revised Primer.

In this book, as in the Revised Primer, I have endeavoured to simplify the marking of quantity by placing the mark of quantity, as a rule, only on the long vowels. It must therefore be noted that vowels not marked are generally to be taken as short, short quantity being only marked where it has seemed necessary to guard against mistake.

B. H. KENNEDY.

The Elms, Cambridge:
  May 1888.

CONTENTS.

THE SHORTER LATIN PRIMER.

LETTERS AND SOUNDS.

1 **The Latin Alphabet** contained twenty-three letters : —

A B C D E F G H I K L M N O P Q R S T V X Y Z.

The sounds which were represented by these twenty-three letters are divided into

      1. Vowels (sounding by themselves);

      2. Consonants (sounding with a vowel).

2   VOWELS.

The vowels were the sounds **a, e, i, o, u,** and of these **i** and **u** were sometimes consonants. We now often write consonant -**i** as **j** (pronounced like English *y* in *yard*), and consonant -**u** as **v** (pronounced like English *w*). [The sound **y** (pronounced like French *u*) occurred only in Greek words, as *lyra*.]

3 **Quantity of Vowels.**—Each of the five vowels could be pronounced either short or long. We in modern times distinguish the short vowels by the sign ˘ and the long vowels by the sign ‾: ămō.

The following is approximately the pronunciation of the vowels :—

    ā (prātum), as **a** in *father*.

    ă (răpit), the same sound shortened, as **a** in *ăliās*.

    ē (mēta), as German **e** in *nehmen*.

    ĕ (frĕta), as **e** in *fret*.

    ī (fīdo), as **ee** in *feed*.

    ĭ (plĭco), as **i** in *fit*.

    ō (nōtus), as Italian **o** in *Roma*.

    ŏ (nŏta), as **o** in *not*.

    ū (tūto), as **oo** in *shoot*.

    ŭ (cŭtis), as **u** in *full*.

Note.—A vowel which is long of itself is called long 'by nature.'
A vowel, naturally short, but coming before two consonants, is long

except where the second consonant is r or l, and is then said to be long 'by position.' A 'vowel before another vowel, or before h, is nearly always short.

4 **Diphthongs.**—A diphthong (double sound) is formed by two vowels coming so close together as to form one syllable. The Latin diphthongs were **ae, au, oe,** and **eu,** pronounced approximately thus :—

 ae (portae), nearly as **ai** in Is*ai*ah.
 au (aurum), as **ou** in h*ou*r.
 oe (poëna), nearly as **oi** in b*oi*l.
 eu (seu), nearly as **ew** in n*ew*.

The Diphthongs are always long.

5 CONSONANTS.

I. **Stops** or **Mutes** (closed consonants) :

(i.) **Velar** or **Guttural** (throat) **q.**

(ii.) **Palatal** (roof of the mouth) { Hard, **c.** / Soft, **g.**

(iii.) **Dental** (teeth) { Hard, **t.** / Soft, **d.**

(iv.) **Labial** (lip) { Hard, **p.** / Soft, **b.**

II. **Spirants** (open consonants), **j** (English y), **s, f, v** (English w).

III. **Liquids, l, r.**

IV. **Nasals, nq, n, m.**

V. The **Aspirate, h.**

x was merely the sign used to represent **cs.**

The pronunciation of the Latin consonants was much the same as that of the English, except that

 1. **c, g, t, s** were always hard :—
 c (cepi, accepi), as **c** in *c*at.
 g (gero, agger), as **g** in *g*et.
 t (fortis, fortia), as **t** in *t*en.
 s (sub, rosa, res), as **s** in *s*it, or as **ce** in ra*ce*.

2. r was always trilled or rolled, even in the middle and at the end of words.

ra*r*us, pa*r*ma, datu*r*.

Doubled Consonants, as in va*cc*a, were pronounced like *kc* in English boo*kc*ase.

z and the three Greek aspirates, **ch, ph, th** are only found in Greek words, as zona, chorus, phalanx, theatrum.

6   **Syllables.**—A syllable consists of a vowel or diphthong either alone or with one or more consonants adjoining it : ĭ-lex, e-ram.

INFLEXION.

7   INFLEXION is a change made in the form of a word to show differences of meaning and use.

The **Stem** is the simplest form of a word in any language before it undergoes changes of Inflexion.

The **Character** is the final sound of the Stem.

The **Root** is the primitive element which the word has in common with kindred words in the same or in other languages.

PARTS OF SPEECH.

8   Words are divided into :

1. NOUNS : which are of three kinds :

Substantives,* names of persons, places, or things :

    Caesar, *Caesar* ; **Rōma,** *Rome* ; **sōl,** *sun* ; **virtūs,** *virtue.*

Adjectives, which express the qualities of Substantives :

    Roma **antīqua,** *ancient Rome* ; sol **clārus,** *the bright sun.*

Pronouns, which stand for a Substantive or Adjective :

    ĕgo, *I* ; **illĕ,** *that, he* ; **mĕŭs,** *my, mine.*

II. VERBS : which express an action or state :

    Sol **dat** lūcem, *the sun gives light* ; Roma **manet,** *Rome remains.*

* In this book the word Noun is often used for Noun Substantive.

III. PARTICLES : which are of four kinds :

Adverbs, which qualify and limit Verbs, Adjectives, and sometimes other Adverbs :

> Roma diu flōruit ; nunc minus potens est.
> *Rome flourished long; now it is less powerful.*

Prepositions, which denote the relation of a Noun to other words in the sentence :

> Per Romam erro, *I wander through Rome.*

Conjunctions, which connect words, phrases, and sentences :

> Caelum suspicio ut lūnam et sīdera videam.
> *I look up to the sky that I may see the moon and stars.*

Interjections : words of exclamation : heu, ēheu, *alas!*

The Parts of Speech are therefore eight :

(1) **Substantives**	(5) **Adverbs**
(2) **Adjectives**	(6) **Prepositions**
(3) **Pronouns**	(7) **Conjunctions**
(4) **Verbs**	(8) **Interjections**
Which have Inflexion.	Which are without Inflexion except the comparison of Adverbs.

9 The Inflexion of Nouns is called Declension ; that of Verbs, Conjugation.

There is no Article in Latin. Lux may stand for *a light, the light,* or simply *light.*

10 Substantives are (*a*) Concrete : vir, *man* ; mensa, *table.* (*b*) Abstract : virtus, *virtue.* Proper names are names of persons or places : Caesar, Roma. A Collective Substantive includes many persons or things of the same kind : turba, *crowd.*

11 Numerals are words which express Number. They are Adjectives, as unus, *one* ; duo, *two* ; or Adverbs, as semel, *once* ; bis, *twice.*

DECLENSION.

12   Declension is the change of form which Nouns undergo to shew changes of **Number and Case.**

13   The NUMBERS are two :

Singular for one person or thing : mensa, *a table* ; gens, *a nation.*

Plural for more than one : mensae, *tables* ; gentēs, *nations.*

14   The CASES are six :

Nominative, the Subject Case, answering the question Who? or What?

Vocative, the Case of one addressed.

Accusative, the Object Case, answering the question Whom? or What?

Genitive, answering the question Of whom? or Of what?

Dative, answering the question To whom? or To what?

Ablative, answering the question From whom? or From what?

Examples of the Cases :

Nominative.	Sol lūcet,	*the sun shines.*
Vocative.	Sol *or* o sol,	*o sun.*
Accusative.	Sōlem lucēre video,	*I see the sun shine.*
Genitive.	Solis lux,	*the sun's light,* or *the light of the sun.*
Dative.	Soli lux addĭtur,	*light is added to the sun.*
Ablative.	Sole lux ēdĭtur,	*light issues from the sun.*

There was in the earliest Latin another Case, called the **Locative,** answering the question Where?

GENDER.

15   The Genders are three :

1, Masculine ; 2, Feminine ; 3, Neuter (*neither*).

Gender is shewn by the form of a word and by its meaning.

Nouns which include both Masculine and Feminine are said to be of Common Gender : cīvis, *citizen* ; auctor, *author.*

(For Memorial Lines on Gender see Appendix.)

16   DECLENSION OF SUBSTANTIVES.

Substantives are grouped in Declensions according to the Character or final letter of the Stem as follows :

(1) FIRST DECLENSION :   A- Stems.

(2) SECOND DECLENSION : O- Stems.

(3) THIRD DECLENSION :   Consonant Stems and I- Stems.

(4) FOURTH DECLENSION : U- Stems.

(5) FIFTH DECLENSION :   E- Stems.

17   The Character of the Stem is most clearly seen before the ending -um or -rum of the Genitive Plural.

The Nominative, masculine and feminine, takes s, except in a- Stems, some Stems in ro- of the Second Declension, and Stems in s, l, r, n, of the Third. The Vocative is like the Nominative, except in the singular of Nouns in -us of the Second Declension.

Neuters have the Accusative like the Nominative in both singular and plural ; the plural always ends in a.

18

FIRST DECLENSION.

A- Stems.

The Nominative Singular is the same as the Stem.

Stem   mensă-
table, f.

	SING.			PLUR.	
Nom.	**mensă,**	*a table.*	**mensae,**	*tables.*
Voc.	**mensa,**	*o table.*	**mensae,**	*o tables.*
Acc.	**mensam,**	*a table.*	**mensās,**	*tables.*
Gen.	**mensae,**	*of a table.*	**mensārum,**	*of tables.*
Dat.	**mensae,**	*to a table.*	**mensīs,**	*to tables.*
Abl.	**mensā,**	*from a table.*	**mensīs,**	*from tables.*

Decline like **mensa**: aquila, *eagle*; lūna, *moon*; rēgīna, *queen*; stella, *star*.

Dea, *goddess,* filia, *daughter,* have Dative and Ablative Plural, deābus, filiābus.

Note.—The Locative sing. ends in **-ae**; the plur. in **-īs**: Romae, *at Rome*; terrae, *on the ground*: mīlitiae, *at the war*: Athēnīs, *at Athens*; foris, *abroad.*

19

SECOND DECLENSION.

O- Stems.

The Nominative is formed from the Stem by adding **s**; in neuter nouns, **m**; the Character ŏ being weakened to ŭ.

In the greater number of nouns whose Stem ends in **ero**, or in **ro** preceded by a stop, the o is dropped, and the Nom. ends in **-er**.

Stem	annŏ- *year*, m.		puĕrŏ- *boy*, m.	măgistrŏ- *master*, m.	bellŏ- *war*, n.
SING.					
Nom.	annŭs,	*a year*	puĕr	magistĕr	bellum
Voc.	annĕ,	*o year*	puĕr	magistĕr	bellum
Acc.	annum,	*a year*	puerum	magistrum	bellum
Gen.	annī,	*of a year*	puerī	magistrī	bellī
Dat.	annō,	*to a year*	puerō	magistrō	bellō
Abl.	annō,	*from a year*	puerō	magistrō	bellō
PLUR.					
Nom.	annī,	*years*	puerī	magistrī	bellă
Voc.	annī,	*o years*	puerī	magistrī	bellă
Acc.	annōs,	*years*	puerōs	magistrōs	bellă
Gen.	annōrum,	*of years*	puerōrum	magistrōrum	bellōrum
Dat.	annīs,	*to years*	puerīs	magistrīs	bellīs
Abl.	annīs,	*from years*	puerīs	magistrīs	bellīs

Decline like **annus**: amīcus, *friend*; dominus, *lord*; servus, *slave*.

Decline like **puer**: gener, *son-in-law*; socer, *father-in-law*; līberī (plur.) *children*; lūcifer, *light-bringer*; armiger, *armour-bearer*.

Decline like **magister**: ager, *field*; cancer, *crab*; līber, *book*.

Decline like **bellum**: regnum, *kingdom*; verbum, *word*.

The following have some exceptional forms :—

Stem	filiŏ-	virŏ-	deŏ-
	son, m.	*man,* m.	*god,* m.
Sing.			
Nom.	filiŭs	vir	deŭs
Voc.	filī	vir	deus
Acc.	filium	virum	deum
Gen.	filii *or* filī	virī	deī
D. Abl.	filiō	virō	deō
Plur.			
N. V.	filiī	virī	dī (dei)
Acc.	filiōs	virōs	deōs
Gen.	filiōrum	virōrum *or* virum	deōrum *or* deum
D. Abl.	filiīs	virīs	dīs (deīs)

Decline like **filius**: Claudius, Vergilius, and many other proper names.

Note.—The Locative singular ends in ī; the plural in īs: humi, *on the ground*; belli, *in time of war*; Milēti, *at Milĕtus*; Phĭlippis, *at Philippi.*

20 **Third Declension.**

Consonant and I- Stems.

The Third Declension contains—

A. Consonant Stems.

> **Stops—**
>
>> (1) Palatals, c, g.
>> (2) Dentals, t, d.
>> (3) Labials, p, b.
>
> **Spirant** s.
> **Nasals**, n, m.
> **Liquids**, l, r.

B. I- Stems.

21 *Syllabus of Consonant Substantives, showing Stem-ending with Nominative and Genitive Singular.*

Stem-ending	Nominative Sing.	Genitive Sing.	English

Stems in Palatals with x in Nom. for cs or gs.

Stem-ending	Nominative Sing.	Genitive Sing.	English
ăc-	fax, f.	făcĭs	*torch*
āc-	pax, f.	pācis	*peace*
ĕc-	nex, f.	nĕcis,	*death*
ĕc- ĭc-	apex, m.	apĭcis	*peak*
ēc-	vervex, m.	vervēcis	*wether*
ĭc-	fornix, m.	fornĭcis	*arch*
ĭc-	jūdex, c.	judĭcis	*judge*
īc-	rādix, f.	radīcis	*root*
ōc-	vox, f.	vōcis	*voice*
ŭc-	dux, c.	dŭcis	*leader*
ūc-	lux, f.	lūcis	*light*
ĕg-	grex, m.	grĕgis	*flock*
ēg-	rex, m.	rēgis	*king*
ĕg- ĭg-	rēmex, m.	remĭgis	*rower*
ĭg-	strix, f.	strĭgis	*screech-owl*
ŭg-	conjunx, c.	conjŭgis	*wife* or *husband*
ūg-	*wanting*	frūgis, f.	*fruit*
ĭv-	nix, f.	nĭvis	*snow*

Stems in Dentals drop t, d, before s in the Nom.

Stem-ending	Nominative Sing.	Genitive Sing.	English
ăt-	ănăs, f.	anătĭs	*duck*
āt-	aetās, f.	aetātis	*age*
ĕt-	sĕgĕs, f.	segĕtis	*corn-crop*
ĕt-	pariĕs, m.	pariĕtis	*room-wall*
ēt-	quiēs, f.	quiētis	*rest*
ĕt- ĭt-	mīlĕs, c.	mīlĭtis	*soldier*
ĭt-	căpŭt, n.	capĭtis	*head*
ōt-	nĕpōs, m.	nepōtis	*grandson*
ūt-	virtūs, f.	virtūtis	*virtue*
ct-	lac, n.	lactis	*milk*
ăd-	văs, m.	vădis	*surety*
ĕd-	pēs, m.	pĕdis	*foot*
ēd-	mercēs, f.	mercēdis	*hire*
aed-	praes, m.	praedis	*bondsman*
ĕd- ĭd-	obsĕs, c.	obsĭdis	*hostage*
ĭd-	lăpĭs, m.	lapĭdis	*stone*
ōd-	custōs, c.	custōdis	*guardian*
ŭd-	pĕcus, f.	pecŭdis	*beast*
ūd-	incūs, f.	incūdis	*anvil*
aud-	laus, f.	laudis	*praise*
rd-	cŏr, n.	cordis	*heart*

Stems in Labials form Nom. regularly with s.

ăp-		wanting	dăpĭs, f.	banquet
ĕp-	ĭp-	princeps, c.	princĭpis	chief
ĭp-		wanting	stĭpis, f.	dole (a small coin)
ŏp-		wanting	ŏpis, f.	help
ĕp-	ŭp-	auceps, m.	aucŭpis	fowler

Stems in the Spirant s, *which, except in* vas, *becomes* r.

ās-		vās, n.	vāsis	vessel
aes-	aer-	aĕs, n.	aeris	copper, bronze
es-	ĕr-	Cerēs, f.	Cĕrĕris	Ceres
ĭs-	ĕr-	cinis, m.	cĭnĕris	cinder
ōs-	ōr-	honōs, m.	honōris	honour
ŏs-	ŏr-	tempŭs, n.	tempŏris	time
ŭs-	ĕr-	opŭs, n.	opĕris	work
ūs-	ūr-	crūs, n.	crūris	leg

Stems in Liquids.

ăl-	sal, m.	sălĭs	salt
ell-	mel, n.	mellis	honey
ĭl-	mūgil, m.	mūgĭlis	mullet
ōl-	sōl, m.	sōlis	sun
ŭl-	consŭl, m.	consŭlis	consul
ăr-	jubăr, n.	jubăris	sunbeam
arr-	far, n.	farris	flour
ĕr-	ansĕr, m.	ansĕris	goose
ēr-	vēr, n.	vēris	spring
ter- tr-	māter, f.	mātris	mother
ŏr-	aequŏr, n.	aequŏris	sea
ŏr-	ĕbŭr, n.	ebŏris	ivory
ōr-	sorŏr, f.	sorōris	sister
ŭr-	vultŭr, m.	vultŭris	vulture
ūr-	fūr, m.	fūris	thief

Stems in Nasals.

ĕn-	ĭn-	nōmĕn, n.	nomĭnis	name
ŏn-	ĭn-	hŏmo, m.	homĭnis	man
ōn-		leo, m.	leōnis	lion
iōn		rătio, f.	ratiōnis	reason
rn-		caro, f.	carnis	flesh
ăn-		cănĭs, c.	canis	dog
ĕn-		juvenĭs, c.	juvenis	young person
ĕm-		hiemps, f.	hiĕmis	winter

A. Consonant Stems.

22   (1) Stems in Palatals: c, g.

Stem	jūdĭc- *judge, c.*		rādīc- *root, f.*	rēg- *king, m.*
SING.				
N. V.	jūdex,	*a judge*	rādix	rex
Acc.	jūdĭcem,	*a judge*	radīcem	rēgem
Gen.	judicĭs,	*of a judge*	radicĭs	regĭs
Dat.	judicī,	*to a judge*	radicī	regī
Abl.	judicĕ,	*from a judge*	radicĕ	regĕ
PLUR.				
N. V.	judicēs,	*judges*	radicēs	regēs
Acc.	judicēs,	*judges*	radicēs	regēs
Gen.	judicum,	*of judges*	radicum	regum
Dat.	judicĭbŭs,	*to judges*	radicĭbŭs	regĭbŭs
Abl.	judicĭbŭs,	*from judges*	radicĭbŭs	regĭbŭs

Decline also: f. vox, **vōc-,** *voice* ; c. dux, dŭc-, *leader* ; m. grex, **grĕg-,** *flock*

23   (2) Stems in Dentals: t, d.

Stem	mīlĭt- *soldier, c.*	pĕd- *foot, m.*	căpĭt- *head, n.*
SING.			
N. V.	mīlĕs	pēs	căpŭt
Acc.	mīlĭtem	pĕdem	capŭt
Gen.	mīlĭtĭs	pedĭs	capĭtĭs
Dat.	mīlĭtī	pedī	capitī
Abl.	mīlĭtĕ	pedĕ	capitĕ
PLUR.			
N. V.	mīlĭtēs	pedēs	capită
Acc.	mīlĭtēs	pedēs	capită
Gen.	mīlĭtum	pedum	capitum
Dat.	mīlĭtĭbŭs	pedĭbŭs	capitĭbŭs
Abl.	mīlĭtĭbŭs	pedĭbŭs	capitĭbŭs

Decline also : f. virtūs, **virtūt-,** *virtue* ; c. sĕgĕs, **segĕt-,** *corn* ; m. lapĭs,
lapĭd-, *stone*

24

(3) Stems in Labials : p, b.

Stem   princĕp-
        princĭp-
        chief, c.

SING.		PLUR.
N. V.	princeps	principēs
Acc.	princĭpem	principēs
Gen.	principĭs	principum
Dat.	principī	principĭbŭs
Abl.	principĕ	principĭbŭs

Decline also : c. forceps, **forcĭp-** , *tongs* ; m. auceps, **aucŭp-**, *fowler.*

25   Stems in the Spirant s.

Stems in **s** do not add **s** in the Nominative Singular, and generally they change **s** into **r** in the other cases.

Stem	flōs- flōr- *flower*, m.	ŏpŭs- ŏpĕr- *work*, n.	crūs- crūr- *leg*, n.
SING.			
N. V.	flōs	opŭs	crūs
Acc.	flōrem	opŭs	crūs
Gen.	florĭs	opĕrĭs	crūrĭs
Dat.	florī	operī	crurī
Abl.	florĕ	operĕ	crurĕ
PLUR.			
N. V.	florēs	operă	crură
Acc.	florēs	operă	crură
Gen.	florum	operum	crurum
Dat.	florĭbŭs	operĭbŭs	crurĭbŭs
Abl.	florĭbŭs	operĭbŭs	crurĭbŭs

Decline also: m. honōs, **honōr-**, *honour* : n. tempus, **tempŏr-**, *time*. corpus, **corpŏr-**, *body* ; genus, genĕr , *race*, jūs, **jūr-**, *law*.

26   Stems in **Liquids**: l, r.

Stems in l, r, do not take s in the Nominative Singular.

Stem	consŭl-	ămŏr-	pătĕr- patr-	aequŏr-
	consul, m.	*love,* m.	*father.*	*sea,* n.
SING.				
N. V.	consŭl	ămŏr	pătĕr	aequŏr
Acc.	consŭlem	amōrem	patrem	aequŏr
Gen.	consŭlĭs	amorĭs	patrĭs	aequŏris
Dat.	consŭlī	amorī	patrī	aequorī
Abl.	consŭlĕ	amorĕ	patrĕ	aequorĕ
PLUR.				
N. V.	consŭlēs	amōrēs	patrēs	aequorā
Acc.	consŭlēs	amōrēs	patrēs	aequorā
Gen.	consŭlum	amōrum	patrum	aequorum
Dat.	consŭlĭbŭs	amorĭbŭs	patrĭbŭs	aequorĭbŭs
Abl.	consŭlĭbŭs	amorĭbŭs	patrĭbŭs	aequorĭbŭs

Decline also: m. sōl, **sōl-,** *sun*; orātŏr, **orātōr-,** *speaker*; carcĕr, **carcĕr-,** *prison*; frāter, **fratr-,** *brother*; n. ebŭr, **ebŏr-,** *ivory*.

27   Stems in **Nasals**: n. m.

Stems ending in **n** do not take **s** in the Nominative Singular.
Stems in ōn, ón, drop the **n.**

Stem	lĕōn-	virgŏn- virgĭn-	nōmĕn- nomin-
	lion, m.	*virgin.* f.	*name,* n.
SING.			
N. V.	leō	vírgō	nōmĕn
Acc.	leōnem	virgĭnem	nomĕn
Gen.	leonĭs	virginĭs	nōmĭnĭs
Dat.	leonī	virginī	nominī
Abl.	leonĕ	virginĕ	nominĕ
PLUR.			
N. V.	leonēs	virginēs	nominā
Acc.	leonēs	virginēs	nominā
Gen.	leonum	virginum	nominum
Dat.	leonĭbŭs	virginĭbŭs	nominĭbŭs
Abl.	leonĭbŭs	virginĭbŭs	nominĭbŭs

Decline also: m. latrō, **latrōn-,** *robber*; f. ratiō, **ratiōn-,** *reason*; m. ordō, **ordĭn-,** *order?* homō, **homĭn-,** *man*; n. carmĕn, **carmĭn-,** *song.*

There is only one Stem in m: hiemps, *winter*: Gen. hiĕmis. f.

B. I- Stems.

28 (1) Stems with Nom. Sing. in -is, and in -er from Stem ri-:

Stem	cīvĭ-	imbrĭ-
	citizen, c.	*shower,* m.
Sing.		
N. V.	cīvĭs	imbĕr
Acc.	civem	imbrem
Gen.	civĭs	imbrĭs
Dat.	civī	imbrī
Abl.	civĕ-ī	imbrĕ-ī
Plur.		
N. V.	civēs	imbrēs
Acc.	civēs	imbrēs
Gen.	civium	imbrium
Dat.	civĭbŭs	imbrĭbŭs
Abl.	civĭbŭs	imbrĭbŭs

Decline like **civis**: m. amnis, *river*; ignis, *fire*; f. avis, *bird*.

Decline like **imber**: f. linter, *boat*; m. ūter, *leathern bottle*.

Note.—Vis, f., *force*, Stem vī-, is thus declined:

	Sing.	**Plur.**
N. V.	vīs	vīres
Acc.	vīm	vīres
Gen.	—	vīrium
Dat.	—	vīribus
Abl.	vī	vīribus

29 (2) Stems with Nom. Sing. in -es :

Stem	nūbĭ- *cloud*, f.	
	Sing.	**Plur.**
N. V.	nūbēs	nubēs
Acc.	nubem	nubēs
Gen.	nubĭs	nubium
Dat.	nubī	nubĭbŭs
Abl.	nubĕ	nubĭbŭs

Decline also : mōlēs, *pile*; rūpēs, *crag*.

30   (3) Stems which have two consonants (a liquid or nasal and a stop) before i, and drop i before the s in the Nom. Sing. :

Stem	montĭ-	urbĭ-
	mountain, m.	*city,* f.
SING.		
N. V.	mons	urbs
Acc.	montem	urbem
Gen.	montĭs	urbĭs
Dat.	montī	urbī
Abl.	montĕ	urbĕ
PLUR.		
N. V.	montēs	urbēs
Acc.	montēs	urbēs
Gen.	montium	urbium
Dat.	montĭbŭs	urbĭbŭs
Abl.	montĭbŭs	urbĭbŭs

Decline also : m. dens, **denti-**, *tooth* ; f. arx, **arci-**, *citadel* ; ars, **arti-**, *art* ; stirps, **stirpi-**, *stem* ; frons, **fronti-**, *forehead* ; frons, **frondi-**, *leaf*.

31   (4) Neuter Stems with Nom. Sing. in -ĕ, -ăl, -ăr :

These either change ĭ into ĕ in the Nom. Sing. or drop the vowel and shorten the final syllable.

Stem	cŭbĭlĭ-	ănĭmālĭ-	calcārĭ-
	couch	*animal*	*spur*
SING.			
N. V. Acc.	cubĭlĕ	animăl	calcăr
Gen.	cubĭlĭs	animālĭs	calcārĭs
Dat. Abl.	cubĭlī	animalī	calcarī
PLUR.			
N. V. Acc.	cubĭliă	animaliă	calcariă
Gen.	cubĭlium	animalium	calcarium
Dat. Abl.	cubĭlĭbŭs	animalĭbŭs	calcarĭbŭs

Decline also : conclāve, *room* ; sedīle, *seat* ; rētĕ, *net* (abl. sing. ĕ) ; mărĕ, *sea* (abl. sing. marī, or more rarely marĕ) ; tribūnal, *tribunal* ; exemplar, *pattern*.

    Note.—The Locative sing. ends in -ī or -ĕ; the plural in -ĭbus : rūrī or rūrĕ, *in the country* ; vesperī or vesperĕ, *in the evening* ; Carthāginī or Carthāginĕ, *at Carthage* ; Gādibus, *at Gades (Cadiz*).

32 With exceptional forms are declined:

		Sing.	Plur.
N. V.	Juppiter	sĕnex (*old man*)	sĕnēs
Acc.	Jŏvem	senem	senēs
Gen.	Jovĭs	senĭs	senum
Dat.	Jovī	senī	senĭbus
Abl.	Jovĕ	senĕ	senĭbus

33   The following rule with regard to the form of the Gen. Plur. may be given for practical convenience:

Nouns with a syllable more in the Gen. Sing. than in the Nom. Sing. (Imparisyllabic Nouns) have Gen. Plur. in -um.

Nouns with the same number of syllables in the Nom. Sing. and Gen. Sing (Parisyllabic Nouns) have Gen. Plur. in -ium.

(For Nouns with irregular Genitive Plural see Appendix, p. 108.)

FOURTH DECLENSION.

34

U- Stems.

The Nominative of masculine and feminine nouns is formed by adding **s**; neuters have the plain Stem with **ū** (long).

Stem	grădŭ-		gĕnŭ
	step, m.		*knee*, n.
Sing.			
Nom.	**grădŭs**	*a step*	gĕnū
Voc.	**gradŭs**	*o step*	genū
Acc.	**gradum**	*a step*	genū
Gen.	**gradūs**	*of a step*	genūs
Dat.	**graduī**	*to a step*	genū
Abl.	**gradū**	*from a step*	genū
Plur.			
Nom.	**gradūs**	*steps*	genŭă
Voc.	**gradūs**	*o steps*	genŭă
Acc.	**gradūs**	*steps*	genŭă
Gen.	**graduum**	*of steps*	genuum
Dat.	**gradĭbŭs**	*to steps*	genĭbŭs
Abl.	**gradĭbŭs**	*from steps*	genĭbŭs

Decline **like gradus**: *m.* fructus, *fruit*; senātus, *senate*; *f.* manus, *hand.*
Decline **like genu**: cornu, *horn*; veru, *spit* (dat. abl. plur. -ĭbus or ŭbus).

Domus, f., is thus declined :

	Singular.	Plural.
N. V.	dŏmŭs	domūs
Acc.	domum	domūs *or* domōs
Gen.	domūs	domōrum *or* domuum
Dat.	domuī *or* domō	domĭbŭs
Abl.	domō	domĭbŭs

The Locative domī, *at home*, is often used.

Fifth Declension.

E- Stems.

35

The Nom. Sing. is formed by adding **s** to the Stem.

Stem rē-, *thing*.

	Singular.			Plural.	
Nom.	rēs	*a thing*		rēs	*things*
Voc.	rēs	*o thing*		rēs	*o things*
Acc.	rem	*a thing*		rēs	*things*
Gen.	rĕī	*of a thing*		rērum	*of things*
Dat.	rĕī	*to a thing*		rēbŭs	*to things*
Abl.	rē	*from a thing*		rēbŭs	*from things*

Decline like **res**: diēs, *day* (gen. dat., diēī); aciēs, *line of battle* ; faciēs, *face* ; seriēs, *series* ; speciēs, *form* ; spēs, *hope* ; fidēs, *faith* ; glaciēs, *ice* ; meridiēs, *noon*.

Res and dies are the only nouns which occur in the Gen., Dat., and Abl. Plural. Fides, meridies, are Singular only.

Note.—The Locative ends in -ē.

Respublica, *the public interest, the republic, the State,* is declined in both its parts :

	Singular.	Plural.
N. V.	rēspublică	rēspublicae
Acc.	rempublicam	rēspublicās
Gen.	reipublicae	rērumpublicārum
Dat.	reipublicae	rēbuspublicīs
Abl.	rēpublică	rēbuspublicīs

DEFECTIVE AND VARIABLE SUBSTANTIVES.

36 Many nouns are found only in the Singular; these are chiefly proper names and words of general meaning: as

justitia,	*justice.*	humus,	*ground.*
vesper,	*evening.*	aurum,	*gold.*

37 Many nouns are used only in the Plural:

arma,	*arms.*	insidiae,	*ambush.*
artūs,	*limbs.*	līberi,	*children.*
cūnae,	*cradle.*	mānes,	*departed spirits.*
dīvitiae,	*riches.*	moenia,	*town walls.*
fasti,	*annals.*	nūgae,	*trifles.*
fēriae,	*holidays.*	penates,	*household gods.*
indūtiae,	*truce.*	tenebrae,	*darkness.*

And names of towns, days, festivals: Athēnae, Delphi, Kalendae *Calends*; Bacchanālia, *festival of Bacchus.*

38 Some words have a different meaning in Singular and Plural.

SINGULAR.		PLURAL.	
aedes,	*temple.*	aedes,	*house.*
aes,	*copper, bronze.*	aera,	*works in bronze.*
auxilium,	*help.*	auxilia,	*allied forces.*
castrum,	*fort.*	castra,	*camp.*
cēra,	*wax.*	cērae,	*waxen tablet.*
cōpia,	*plenty.*	cōpiae,	*forces.*
fīnis,	*end.*	fines,	*boundaries.*
grātia,	*favour.*	gratiae,	*thanks.*
impedīmentum,	*hindrance.*	impedimenta,	*baggage.*
littera,	*letter of the alphabet.*	litterae,	*epistle, literature.*
lūdus,	*play.*	ludi,	*public games.*
opem (acc.),	*help.*	opes,	*wealth.*
sal,	*salt.*	sales,	*wit.*

39 Some nouns have two forms of Declension:

pecus, pecŏris, n., *cattle*; pecus, pecŭdis, f., *a single head of cattle*; plebs, plēbis, f.; plebes, plebei, f., *the common people.*

40 In many nouns some of the cases are wanting; thus:

	feast, f.,	*fruit*, f.,	*help*, f.,	*prayer*, f.,	*change*, f.
N. V.	—	—	—	—	—
Acc.	dăpem	frūgem	ŏpem	prĕcem	vīcem
Gen	dapĭs	frugĭs	opĭs	—	vicĭs
Dat.	dapī	frugī	—	precī	—
Abl.	dapĕ	frugĕ	opĕ	precĕ	vicĕ

These have full plural -es, -um, -ibus, except Gen. vicium.

41 Some have only Nom. Acc. Sing.: fās, *right*, nĕfās, *wrong*, instar, *likeness, size.*

Nemo, *nobody*, has only Acc. neminem, Dat. nemini. (69.)

DECLENSION OF ADJECTIVES.

42 Adjectives are declined by Gender, Number and Case.

43 A. Adjectives of three endings in -us, -a, -um or -er, -a, -um are declined like Substantives of the Second and First Declension, O- and A- Stems.

Stem	bŏnŏ-	bŏnă	bŏnŏ-
		good.	

SING.	M.	F.	N.
Nom.	bonŭs	bonă	bonum
Voc.	bonĕ	bonă	bonum
Acc.	bonum	bonam	bonum
Gen.	bonī	bonae	bonī
Dat.	bonō	bonae	bonō
Abl.	bonō	bonā	bonō

PLURAL.			
Nom.	bonī	bonae	bonă
Voc.	bonī	bonae	bonă
Acc.	bonōs	bonās	bonă
Gen.	bonōrum	bonārum	bonōrum
Dat.	bonīs	bonīs	bonīs
Abl.	bonīs	bonīs	bonīs

Decline also: cārus, *dear*; dūrus, *hard*; malus, *bad*; magnus, *great*; parvus, *small*; dubius, *doubtful.*

Stem	tĕnĕrŏ-	tĕnĕrā-	tĕnĕrŏ-
		tender.	

SING.	M.	F.	N.
Nom.	tenĕr	tenĕrā	tenĕrum
Voc.	tener	tenerā	tenerum
Acc.	tenerum	teneram	tenerum
Gen.	tenerī	tenerae	tenerī
Dat.	tenerō	tenerae	tenerō
Abl.	tenerō	tĕnerā	tenerō

PLURAL.			
N. V.	tenerī	tenerae	tenerā
Acc.	tenerōs	tenerās	tenerā
Gen.	tenerōrum	tenerārum	tenerōrum
D., Abl.	tenerīs	tenerīs	tenerīs

Decline also: asper, *rough*; lacer, *torn*; līber, *free*; miser, *wretched*; prosper, *prosperous*; frūgifer, *fruit-bearing*, plūmiger, *feathered*, and other compounds of fero and gero; also satur, *full*, satūra, satūrum.

Stem	nĭgrŏ-	nĭgrā-	nĭgrŏ-
		black.	

SING.	M.	F.	N.
Nom.	nĭgĕr	nĭgrā	nĭgrum
Voc.	nigĕr	nigrā	nigrum
Acc.	nigrum	nigram	nigrum
Gen.	nigrī	nigrae	nigrī
Dat.	nigrō	nigrae	nigrō
Abl.	nigrō	nigrā	nigrō

PLURAL.			
N. V.	nigrī	nigrae	nigrā
Acc.	nigrōs	nigrās	nigrā
Gen.	nigrōrum	nigrārum	nigrōrum
D., Abl.	nigrīs	nigrīs	nigrīs

Decline also: aeger, *sick*; āter, *jet-black*; pulcher, *beautiful*; ruber, *red*; sacer, *sacred*.

44   B. Adjectives of two endings and of one ending in the Nominative Singular are declined like Substantives of the Third Declension.

45   (1) Adjectives with Nominative Singular in **-is**, Masc. and Fem.; in **-e** Neuter: I- Stems.

Stem   tristĭ-, *sad.*

	SINGULAR.		PLURAL.	
	M. F.	N.	M. F.	N.
N. V.	tristĭs	tristĕ	tristēs	tristiă
Acc.	tristem	tristĕ	tristēs, -īs	tristiă
Gen.	tristĭs	tristĭs	tristium	tristium
D., Abl.	tristī	tristī	tristĭbŭs	tristĭbŭs

Decline also: brĕvis, *short*; omnis, *all*; aequālis, *equal*; hostīlis, *hostile*; acilis, *easy*; illustris, *illustrious*; lūgubris, *mournful.*

Some stems in **ri-** form the Masc. Nom. Sing. in **-er**:

Stem   ācrĭ-, *keen.*

SING.	M.	F.	
N. V.	ācĕr	ācrĭs	ācrĕ
Acc.	acrem	acrem	acrĕ
Gen.	acrĭs	acrĭs	acrĭs
Dat.	acrī	acrī	acrī
Abl.	acrī	acrī	acrī

PLUR.			
N. V.	acrēs	acrēs	acriă
Acc.	acrēs, -īs	acrēs, -īs	acriă
Gen.	acrium	acrium	acrium
D., Abl.	acrĭbŭs	acrĭbŭs	acrĭbŭs

Decline like acer the following: celĕber, *famous*; salūber, *healthy*; alăcer, *brisk*; campester, *level*; equester. *equestrian*; pedester, *pedestrian*; paluster, *marshy*; puter, *crumbling.*

Note.—Names of months are masculine in form (agreeing with mensis, understood): Aprilis is declined like tristis: September, October, November, December like acer: the rest like bonus.

46   (2) Adjectives with Nom. Sing. the same for all genders:

   (a) *I- Stems.*

Stem   fēlĭcĭ-, *happy*.

	M. F. SING.	N.	M. F. PLUR.	N.
N. V.	felix	felix	felicēs	feliciă
Acc.	felīcem	felix	felicēs, -īs	feliciă
Gen.	felicĭs	felicĭs	felicium	felicium
Dat.	felicī	felicī	felicĭbŭs	felicĭbŭs
Abl.	felicī	felicī	felicĭbŭs	felicĭbŭs

Stem   ingentĭ-, *huge*.

	M. F. SING.	N.	M. F. PLUR.	N.
N. V.	ingens	ingens	ingentēs	ingentiă
Acc.	ingentem	ingens	ingentēs, -īs	ingentiă
Gen.	ingentĭs		ingentium	
Dat.	ingentī		ingentĭbŭs	
Abl.	ingentī		ingentĭbŭs	

Decline like **felix**: audax, audāci-, *bold*; duplex, duplici-, *double*; vēlox, velōci-, *swift*.

Decline like **ingens**: amans, amanti-, *loving*; sapiens, sapienti-, *wise*; concors, concordi-, *agreeing*; păr, pări-, *like*.

47   (b) *Consonant Stems.*

   Stem   dīvĭt-, *rich*.

	SINGULAR.	PLURAL.
N. V.	dīvĕs	dīvitēs
Acc.	divĭtem	divitēs
Gen.	divitĭs	divitum
Dat.	divitī	divitĭbŭs
Abl.	divitĕ	divitĭbŭs

Decline like dives: pauper, pauper-, *poor*; dēgener, degener-, *degenerate*; sospes, sospit-, *safe*; superstes, superstit-, *surviving*; deses, desid-, *slothful*; compos, compot-, *possessing*; caelebs, caelib-, *unmarried*; vetus, veter-, *old*.

Dives has a contracted form dīs, acc. ditem, &c.; with abl. sing. diti and neut. plur. dītia; gen. plur. ditium. Dives, vetus, and superstes are used as neut. nom., voc., and acc. sing. Vetus has neut. plur. vetera. The rest have no neuter forms.

COMPARISON OF ADJECTIVES.

48   Adjectives are compared in three degrees.

    (1) Positive :   dŭrus, *hard.*   **tristis,** *sad.*
    (2) Comparative : durĭŏr, *harder.*   **tristĭŏr,** *sadder.*
    (3) Superlative : durissĭmus, *hardest.*   **tristissĭmus,** *saddest.*

The Positive is the adjective itself expressing the quality; the Comparative expresses a greater degree; the Superlative expresses a very great, or the greatest, degree of the quality.

The Comparative is formed from the Positive by adding the suffix -ior to the last consonant of the Stem; the Superlative generally by adding -issimus to the last consonant of the Stem.

Stem	Positive	Comparative	Superlative
dur-o-	durus	dur-iŏr	dur-issimus
trist-i-	tristis	trist-iŏr	trist-issimus
audāc-i-	audax, *bold*	audac-iŏr	audac-issimus

49   The Comparative is declined as follows :

	M. F. SING. N.		M. F. PLUR. N.	
N. V.	tristior	tristius	tristiōrēs	tristiōră
Acc.	tristiōrem	tristius	tristior-es	tristioră
Gen.	tristiōrĭs		tristiorum	
Dat.	tristiorī		tristiorĭbŭs	
Abl.	tristior-ĕ, -ī*		tristiorĭbŭs	

50   The Superlative is declined from o- and a- Stems, like bonus.

Adjectives with Stems in **ro-, ri-,** form the Superlative by doubling the last consonant of the Stem and adding **-imus.** Words like niger insert e before r in the Superlative.

Stem	Positive	Comparative	Superlative
tener-o-	tener, *tender*	tenerior	tenerrĭmus
nigr-o-	niger, *black*	nigrior	nigerrĭmus
celer-i-	celer, *swift*	celerior	celerrĭmus

---

* The Ablative in -ī is rare.

Six adjectives with Stems in ĭli- also form the Superlative by doubling the last consonant of the Stem and adding -imus :

| facilis, *easy.* | similis, *like.* | gracilis, *slender.* |
| difficilis, *difficult.* | dissimilis, *unlike.* | humilis, *lowly.* |

| facil-i · | facilis | facilior | facillimus |

Irregular Comparison.

51 (1) Some Comparatives and Superlatives are formed from Stems distinct from that of the Positive :

Positive		Comparative		Superlative
bonus,	*good.*	melior,	*better.*	optimus, *best.*
malus,	*bad.*	pējor,	*worse,*	pessimus, *worst.*
parvus,	*small.*	minor,	*less.*	minimus, *least.*
multus,	*much.*	plūs,	*more.*	plūrimus, *most.*
magnus,	*great.*	mājor,	*greater.*	maximus, *greatest.*

Plūs in the Singular is neuter only :

	Sing.	m. f.	Plur.	n.
N. V. Acc.	plūs	plūres		plūra
Gen.	pluris		plurium	
Dat.	——		pluribus	
Abl.	plurĕ		pluribus	

Senex, *old,* has Comp. senior *or* nātu mājor ; Superl. nātu maximus. Natu major quam ego : *older than I.*

Juvenis, *young,* has Comp. jūnior *or* nātu minor ; Superl. nātu minimus.

> Note 1.—Senior, junior are **not** used as true comparatives of senex, juvenis, but with the meaning *old* (*rather than young*), and *young* (*rather than old*).
> Note 2.—Dives, *rich,* has two forms : divitior and dītior ; divitissimus and ditissimus.
> Vetus, *old,* has vetustior (veterior), veterrimus.

52 (2) Adjectives compounded with -dĭcus, -fĭcus, -vŏlus (from dīco, facio, volo), form the Comparative and Superlative as if from participles in -ens.

Positive	Comparative	Superlative
maledĭcus, *evil-speaking.*	maledĭcentior	maledĭcentissimus
benefĭcus, *beneficent.*	beneficentior	beneficentissimus
benevŏlus, *well-wishing.*	benevolentior	benevolentissimus

53   (3) Adjectives in -eus, -ius, -uus are generally compared by using the adverbs magis, *more*, maxime, *most*, with the Positive: dubius, *doubtful*, magis dubius, *more doubtful*, maxime dubius, *most doubtful*.

54   Some Comparatives and Superlatives denoting relations of place have no Positive, but correspond to Adverbs from the same Stem.

	Comparative Adj	Superlative Adj.
extrā (adv.), *outside*.	extĕrior	extrēmus, extĭmus
intrā (adv.), *within*.	intĕrior	intĭmus
suprā (adv.), *above*.	supĕrior	suprēmus, summus
infrā (adv.), *below*.	infĕrior	infĭmus, īmus
citrā (adv.), *on this side*.	citĕrior	citĭmus
ultrā (adv.), *beyond*.	ultĕrior	ultĭmus
prae (prep.), *before*.	prior	prīmus, *first*.
post (prep.), *after*.	postĕrior	postrēmus, *last*.
prŏpĕ (adv.), *near*.	propior	proximus

COMPARISON OF ADVERBS.

55   Adverbs derived from adjectives and ending in -ē, -ō, -ter, and rarely -ĕ, form Comparative in -ius, Superlative in -issimē.

Adjective	Adverb	Comparative	Superlative
dignus, *worthy*.	dignē, *worthily*.	dignius	dignissimē
tūtus, *safe*.	tūtō, *safely*.	tutius	tutissimē
fortis, *brave*.	fortiter, *bravely*.	fortius	fortissimē
facilis, *easy*.	facilĕ, *easily*.	facilius	facillimē

56   Irregular Comparison has corresponding forms in Adverbs.

Adverb	Comparative	Superlative
benĕ, *well*.	melius	optimē
malĕ, *ill*.	pējus	pessimē
paullum, *little*.	minus	minimē
multum, *much*.	plūs	plūrimum
magnŏpĕre, *greatly*.	magis	maximē
diū, *long*.	diutius	diutissimē
intus, *within*.	intĕrius	intimē

Magis means *more* in degree; plus, *more* in quantity.

NUMERALS.

57   Numeral Adjectives are of three kinds :
1. Cardinals ; answering the question, *How many ?*
2. Ordinals ; answering the question, *Which in order of number ?*
3. Distributives ; answering the question, *How many each ?*

58   Numeral Adverbs answer the question, *How many times ?*
Unus, from o- and a- Stems, is declined as follows :

	Sing.			Plur.		
Nom.	ūnus	ūna	ūnum	ūnī	ūnae	ūnă
Acc.	unum	unam	unum	unōs	unās	una
Gen.	unius	unius	unius	unorum	unarum	unorum
Dat.	unī	unī	unī	unīs	unīs	unīs
Abl.	unō	unā	unō	unīs	unīs	unīs

Duŏ is an o- Stem, and trēs an i- Stem.

	M.	F.	N.	M. and F.	
Nom.	duŏ	duae	duŏ	trēs	tria
Acc.	duōs, duo	duās	duo	trēs	tria
Gen.	duōrum	duārum	duōrum	trium	trium
D., Abl.	duōbŭs	duābŭs	duōbŭs	trĭbŭs	trĭbŭs

Decline like **duŏ** : ambō, *both.*

The Cardinals from quattuor to centum are indeclinable.
Hundreds from *two* to *nine hundred* are o- and a- Stems,
ducentī, ducentae, ducenta. Mille (*a thousand*) is an indeclinable
adjective ; but mīlia (*thousands*) is a neuter substantive, declined
like animalia. Mille passus, *a mile.*

In Compound Numbers above twenty, the order is the same
as in English. Either the smaller number with **et** comes first,
or the larger without **et** : septem et trīginta, *seven and thirty* ;
or trīginta septem, *thirty-seven.* Unus usually stands first : unus
et vīgintī, *twenty-one.* In numbers above a hundred the larger
comes first, with or without **et.**

Thousands are expressed by putting (1) the numeral adverbs
bis, ter, &c., before mille : bis mille ; or (2) cardinal numbers before mīlia : duo mīlia.

Mīlia is followed by a genitive : duo mīlia hominum, *two
thousand men.*

59 Arabic Numerals	Roman Numerals	Cardinals; answering the question Quot? how many?	Ordinals; answering the question Quotus? which in order of number? m. -ŭs, f. -ă, n. -um.	Distributives; answering the question Quotēni? how many each? m. -ī, f. -ae, n. -ă.	Numeral Adverbs; answering the question Quotiens? how many times?
1	I	ūnus	prīmus (prior), first	singŭlī, one each	semel, once
2	II	duo	secundus (alter), second	bīnī, two each	bis, twice
3	III	trēs	tertius, third, &c.	ternī, or trīnī, three each, &c.	ter, three times, &c.
4	IIII or IV	quattuor	quartus	quaternī	quater
5	V	quinque	quintus	quīnī	quinquiens
6	VI	sex	sextus	sēnī	sexiens
7	VII	septem	septĭmus	septēnī	septiens
8	VIII or IIX	octo	octāvus	octōnī	octiens
9	VIIII or IX	nŏvem	nōnus	novēnī	noviens
10	X	dĕcem	decĭmus	dēnī	deciens
11	XI	undĕcim	undecimus	undēnī	undeciens
12	XII	duodecim	duodecimus	duodēnī	duodeciens
13	XIII	tredecim	tertius decimus	ternī dēnī	tredeciens
14	XIIII or XIV	quattuordecim	quartus decimus	quaternī dēnī	quattuordeciens
15	XV	quindecim	quintus decimus	quīnī dēnī	quindeciens
16	XVI	sēdecim	sextus decimus	sēnī dēnī	sēdeciens
17	XVII	septemdecim	septimus decimus	septēnī dēnī	septiesdeciens
18	XVIII or XIIX	{ duŏdēvīgintī / octodecim	duodēvīcensimus	duodēvīceni	duodēvīciens

	Cardinal	Ordinal	Distributive	Adverbial
19	XVIIII or XIX	undēvīginti / novendecim	undēvīcensimus	undēvīcēnī	undēvīciens
20	XX	vīgintī	vīcensimus	vīcēnī	vīciens
21	XXI	unus et vīginti	unus et vīcensimus	vīcēnī singuli	semel et vīciens
22	XXII	duo et vīginti	alter et vīcensimus	vīcēnī bini	bis et vīciens
30	XXX	trīginta	trigensimus	trīcēnī	trīciens
40	XXXX or XL	quādrāgintā	quādrāgensimus	quādrāgēnī	quādrāgiens
50	L	quīnquāginta	quīnquāgensimus	quīnquāgēnī	quīnquāgiens
60	LX	sexāginta	sexāgensimus	sexāgēnī	sexāgiens
70	LXX	septuāginta	septuāgensimus	septuāgēnī	septuāgiens
80	LXXX or XXC	octōginta	octōgensimus	octōgēnī	octōgiens
90	LXXXX or XC	nōnāginta	nōnāgensimus	nōnāgēnī	nōnāgiens
100	C	centum	centensimus	centēnī	centiens
101	CI	centum et unus	centensimus primus	centēni singuli	centiens semel
200	CC	ducentī, ae, a	ducentensimus	ducēnī	ducentiens
300	CCC	trecenti	trecentensimus	trecēnī	trecentiens
400	CCCC	quadringenti	quadringentensimus	quadringēnī	quadringentiens
500	IƆ or D	quingenti	quingentensimus	quingēnī	quingentiens
600	IƆC	sexcenti	sexcentensimus	sēcēnī	sexcentiens
700	IƆCC	septingenti	septingentensimus	septingēnī	septingentiens
800	IƆCCC	octingenti	octingentensimus	octingēnī	octingentiens
900	IƆCCCC	nongenti, noning.	nongentensimus	nongēnī	nongentiens
1,000	CIƆ or M	millē	millensimus	singula milia	miliens
2,000	CIƆCIƆ or MM	duo milia	bis-millensimus	bina milia	bis miliens

PRONOUNS.

60   Pronouns either stand in the place of Substantives, or stand in the place of Adjectives, to define or point out Substantives.

There are three Persons :

First : The person speaking : *I* or *we*.
Second : The person spoken to : *thou* or *ye* (*you*).
Third : The person or thing spoken of : *he, she, it, they*

Personal Pronouns stand only in place of Substantives. Possessive Pronouns, as meus, *my*, are used only as Adjectives. Most of the others can stand for Substantives or Adjectives.

61   Personal and Reflexive.

Singular.

	1st Person.		2nd Person.	
Nom.	ĕgŏ,	*I.*	tū,	*thou* (so also Voc.)
Acc.	mē,	*me.*	tē,	*thee.*
Gen.	meī,	*of me.*	tuī,	*of thee.*
Dat.	mĭhĭ,	*to me.*	tĭbĭ,	*to thee.*
Abl.	mē,	*from me.*	tē,	*from thee.*

Plural.

	1st Person.		2nd Person.	
Nom.	nōs,	*we.*	vōs,	*ye* (so also Voc.)
Acc.	nōs,	*us.*	vōs,	*you.*
Gen.	{nostrī / nostrum},	*of us.*	{vestrī / vestrum},	*of you.*
Dat.	nōbīs,	*to us.*	vōbīs,	*to you.*
Abl.	nōbīs,	*from us.*	vōbīs,	*from you.*

Reflexive Pronoun.

Nom.	—	
Acc.	sē or sēsē,	*himself, herself, itself,* or *themselves.*
Gen.	suī,	*of himself, &c.*
Dat.	sĭbĭ,	*to himself, &c.*
Abl.	sē or sēsē,	*from himself, &c.*

For the Personal Pronoun of the 3rd Person, *he, she, it,* the **Demonstrative** is, ea, id, is used.

62

POSSESSIVE.

Sing.
1st Person : **meŭs, meă, meum,** *my.*
2nd Person : **tuŭs, tuă, tuum,** *thy.*

Plur.
1st Person : **nostĕr, nostră, nostrum,** *our.*
2nd Person : **vestĕr, vestră, vestrum,** *your.*

Suus, sua, suum, *his, her, its, their,* is the Possessive of the Reflexive Pronoun.

Meus, tuus, suus are declined like bonus : noster, vester, like niger. Meus has Voc. Sing. masc. mī. The other Possessives, except noster, have no Vocative.

63

DEMONSTRATIVE.

Is, *that,* or *he, she, it.*

	SINGULAR.			PLURAL.		
	M.	**F.**	**N.**	**M.**	**F.**	**N.**
Nom.	ĭs	eă	ĭd	iī *or* eī	eae	eă
Acc.	eum	eam	id	eōs	eās	eă
Gen.	ējŭs	ējŭs	ējŭs	eōrum	eārum	eōrum
Dat.	eī	eī	eī	iīs (eīs)	iīs (eīs)	iīs (eīs)
Abl.	eō	eā	eō	iīs (eīs)	iīs (eīs)	iīs (eīs)

Hic, *this* (*near me*), or *he, she, it.*

	SINGULAR.			PLURAL.		
	M.	**F.**	**N.**	**M.**	**F.**	**N.**
Nom.	hīc	haec	hōc	hī	hae	haec
Acc.	hunc	hanc	hoc	hōs	hās	haec
Gen.	hūjus	hūjus	hūjus	hōrum	hārum	hōrum
Dat.	huic	huic	huic	hīs	hīs	hīs
Abl.	hōc	hāc	hōc	hīs	hīs	hīs

Ille, *that* (*yonder*), or *he, she, it.*

	SINGULAR.			PLURAL.		
	M.	**F.**	**N.**	**M.**	**F.**	**N.**
Nom.	illĕ	illă	illŭd	illī	illae	illă
Acc.	illum	illam	illud	illōs	illās	illă
Gen.	illĭus	illĭus	illĭus	illōrum	illārum	illōrum
Dat.	illī	illī	illī	illīs	illīs	illīs
Abl.	illō	illā	illō	illīs	illīs	illīs

Istĕ, *that* (*near you*), is declined like ille.

DEFINITIVE.

64

Idem, *same.*

SINGULAR.

	M.	F.	N.
Nom.	īdem	eădem	ĭdem
Acc.	eundem	eandem	idem
Gen.	ējusdem	ējusdem	ējusdem
Dat.	eīdem	eīdem	eīdem
Abl.	eōdem	eădem	eōdem

PLURAL.

Nom.	eīdem *or* īdem	eaedem	eădem
Acc.	eosdem	easdem	eadem
Gen.	eōrundem	eārundem	eōrundem
Dat.		eīsdem *or* īsdem	
Abl.		eīsdem *or* īsdem	

Ipsĕ, *self.*

	SINGULAR.			PLURAL.		
	M.	F.	N.	M.	F.	N.
Nom.	ipsĕ	ipsă	ipsum	ipsī	ipsae	ipsă
Acc.	ipsum	ipsam	ipsum	ipsōs	ipsas	ipsă
Gen.	ipsĭus	ipsĭus	ipsĭus	ipsōrum	ipsārum	ipsōrum
Dat.	ipsī	ipsī	ipsī	ipsīs	ipsīs	ipsīs
Abl.	ipsō	ipsā	ipsō	ipsīs	ipsīs	ipsīs

65

RELATIVE.

Qui, *who, which.*

	SINGULAR.			PLURAL.		
	M.	F.	N.	M.	F.	N.
Nom.	quĭ	quae	quŏd	quī	quae	quae
Acc.	quem	quam	quod	quōs	quās	quae
Gen.	cūjŭs	cūjŭs	cūjŭs	quōrum	quārum	quōrum
Dat.	cuĭ	cuī	cuī	quĭbŭs *or* quīs		
Abl.	quō	quā	quō	quĭbŭs *or* quīs		

66

INTERROGATIVE.

Quis, *who ? what ?*

	M.	F.	N.		M.	F.	A.
Nom.	quĭs / quī	(quĭs) / quae	quĭd / quŏd	*Acc.*	quem / quem	quam / quam	quĭd / quŏd

In all other Cases singular and plural qui Interrogative is like the Relative.

67

INDEFINITE.

Quis, *anyone* or *anything*.

	M.	F.	N.			M.	F.	N.
Nom. {	quĭs	quă	quĭd		*Acc.* {	quem	quam	quĭd
	quī	quae	quŏd			quem	quam	quŏd

In all other Cases the Indefinite is like the Relative, except that quă or quae may be used in neut. nom. and acc. plural.

Quis, both Interrogative and Indefinite, and its compounds, are used **chiefly** as Substantives; **qui** and its compounds **chiefly** as Adjectives.

Quid and its compounds are used **only** as Substantives; **quod** and its compounds **only** as Adjectives.

> EXAMPLES:
>
> | Homo qui venit, | *The man who comes.* | (qui, relative.) |
> |---|---|---|
> | Quis venit ? | *Who comes ?* | (quis, interrogative.) |
> | Qui homo venit ? | *What man comes ?* | (qui, interrogative.) |
> | Aliquid amari, | *Some bitterness.* | |
> | Aliquod verbum, | *Some word.* | |

68

COMPOUND PRONOUNS.

MASC.	FEM.	NEUT.	
quīcumquĕ,	quaecumquĕ,	quodcumquĕ,	} *whosoever*, or
quisquĭs,	quisquĭs,	quidquĭd or quicquĭd,	} *whatsoever.*
quīdam,	quaedam,	quiddam (quoddam),	{ *a certain person* or *thing.*
ălĭquĭs,	ălĭquă,	ălĭquid,	} *someone* or
aliquī,	aliquă,	aliquod,	} *something.*
quisquam,	——	quidquam or quicquam,	{ *anyone at all.*
quisquĕ,	quaequĕ,	quidquĕ (quodque),	{ *each one severally*
ŭterquĕ,	utraquĕ,	utrumquĕ,	*each of two*

Quisquam is used as a Substantive, sing. only, chiefly in negative sentences; and the Adjective which corresponds to it is **ullus**: haud quisquam, *not anyone.*

69   The following Pronominal Adjectives form the Gen. Sing. in
-ius and the Dat. Sing. in -ī like ille : alius, *other, another* ;
ullus, *any* ; nullus, *none*; sōlus, *sole* ; tōtus, *whole* ; ŭter, *which
of two* ; alter, *one of two, the other* ; neuter, *neither.*

SINGULAR.   PLURAL.

	M.	F.	N.	M.	F.	N.
Nom.	ălĭŭs	ălĭă	ălĭŭd	ălĭī	ăliae	ălĭă
Acc.	alium	aliam	ălĭŭd	aliōs	aliās	alĭa
Gen.	alīŭs	alīŭs	alīŭs	aliōrum	aliārum	aliōrum
Dat.	alĭī	alĭī	alĭī	aliīs	aliīs	aliīs
Abl.	aliō	aliā	aliō	aliīs	aliīs	aliīs

Note.—In alius the i of the Gen. Sing. is always long. In the
Gen. of words declined like it the quantity of the i is doubtful; also
in the Gen. of uter, neuter.

Like alius, but with Neuter Singular in -um, are declined
ullus, nullus, sōlus, tōtus.

Nullius, Gen. Sing. and nullo, Abl. Sing. of nullus are used
for the Gen. and Abl. of nemo, nobody.   (41).

SINGULAR.

	M.	F.	N.
Nom.	altĕr	altĕră	altĕrum
Acc.	altĕrum	altĕram	altĕrum
Gen.	alterĭŭs	alterĭŭs	alterĭŭs
Dat.	alterī	alterī	alterī
Abl.	alterō	alterā	alterō

PLURAL.

	M.	F.	N.
Nom.	altĕrī	altĕrae	altĕră
Acc.	alterōs	alterās	altĕră
Gen.	alterōrum	alterārum	alterōrum
Dat.	alterīs	alterīs	alterīs
Abl.	alterīs	alterīs	alterīs

Like alter, but casting out e before **r** in all cases except the
Nom. Sing. Masculine, are declined,—

ūter, utra, utrum, *which (of two).*   neuter, neutra, neutrum,
neither.   These are seldom used in the plural.

VERBS.

70

The **Verb** has:

The **Three Persons**—First, Second, Third.
The **Two Numbers**—Singular and Plural.
Six Tenses:
    (1) Present, (2) Future Simple, (3) Past
        Imperfect, (4) Perfect or Aorist,
        (5) Future Perfect, (6) Pluperfect.
Three Moods:
    (1) Indicative, (2) Imperative, (3) Sub-
        junctive.

} The Verb Finite.

The **Infinitive** (Verbal Substantive).
Three Participles (Verbal Adjectives).
The **Gerund** and **Gerundive** (Verbal Substantive
    and Adjective).
Two Supines (Verbal Substantives).

} The Verb Infinite.

Two Voices:

    (1) Active, (2) Passive.

The Verb Finite is so called because it is limited by Mood
and Persons; while the Verb Infinite is not so limited.

71 PERSON AND NUMBER.

In English, Pronouns are used with Verbs to express the three Persons Singular and Plural: *I am. We are.* But in Latin the Pronouns are expressed by the personal suffixes.

su-m,	*I am,* am-o, *I love.*	su-mus,	*we are.*
e-s,	*thou art (you are).*	es-tis,	*ye are.*
es-t,	*he (she, it) is.*	su-nt,	*they are.*

The Imperative Mood has only the Second and Third Person Singular and Plural, not the First.

72 TENSES.

Tenses express the time of the action or state denoted by the Verb, as being:

    (1) Present, Past, or Future;
    (2) Complete or Incomplete;
    (3) Momentary or Continuous.

In English, by means of auxiliary Verbs, differences of time can be more accurately expressed than in Latin; so that one tense in Latin may correspond to two tenses in English. Thus, rogo, *I ask,* has the following tenses:

Present	Present	*incomplete*	rogo	*I ask* / *I am asking*
	Perfect	*complete*	rogavi	*I have asked* / *I have been asking*
Future	Fut. Simple	*incomplete*	rogabo	*I shall ask* / *I shall be asking*
	Fut. Perf.	*complete*	rogavero	*I shall have asked* / *I shall have been asking*
Past	Perfect } Imperfect }	*incomplete*	rogavi } rogabam }	*I had asked* / *I was asking*
	Pluperf.	*complete*	rogaveram	*I had asked* / *I had been asking*

The Present, the Future Simple, and the Future Perfect are called **Primary** Tenses.

The Imperfect and the Pluperfect are called **Historic** Tenses.

The Perfect in the sense of *I have loved* is **Primary**; in the sense of *I loved* it is **Historic**.

73   MOOD.

Moods are the forms in which the idea contained in the Verb is presented.

The **Indicative** is the mood which states a fact: amo, *I love.*

The **Imperative** is the mood of command: amā, *love thou.*

The **Subjunctive** is the mood which represents something as thought of or as dependent: ut amem, *that I may love*; si amarem, *if I were to love.** It has no Future tense-forms, but its other tenses sometimes have future meaning, or Periphrastic Conjugation is used.

74   THE VERB INFINITE.

The **Infinitive** is a Verb Noun expressing action or state in general, without limit of person or number: amāre, *to love*: amavisse, *to have loved*; amāri, *to be loved.*

The **Gerund** is a Verbal Substantive declined like neuters of the Second Declension. It supplies Cases to the Infinitive: as amandi, *of loving.*

The **Gerundive** is a Participle, or Verbal Adjective: amandus, a, um, *meet to be loved.*

The **Supines** are Cases of a Verbal Substantive: amātum, *in order to love*; amātu, *for* or *in loving.*

The **Participles** are so called because they have partly the properties of Verbs and partly those of Adjectives; there are three besides the Gerundive:

(*a*) Act. Pres. amans,   *loving* (declined like ingens).
(*b*) Act. Fut. amatūrus, *about to love*⎫ (declined like
(*c*) Pass. Perf. amātus, *loved*   ⎭ bonus).

---

* In the Paradigms the tenses of the Subjunctive are given without any English translation, because their meaning varies so much according to the context that it is impossible to convey it by any one rendering.

75 VOICE.

The **Active Voice** expresses what the Subject of a Verb is or does :

sum, *I am* ; valeo, *I am well* ; amō, *I love* ; regō, *I rule.*

The **Passive Voice** expresses what is done to the Subject of the Verb :

amor, *I am loved* ; regor, *I am ruled.*

76 **Deponent Verbs** are Verbs which have chiefly the forms of the Passive Voice with the meaning of the Active Voice.

77 Verbs in the Active Voice and Deponent Verbs are,

(*a*) Transitive, having a direct object :
amo eum, *I love him* ; hortor vōs, *I exhort you.*

(*b*) Intransitive, not having a direct object : stō, *I stand* ; loquor, *I speak.*

Only Transitive Verbs have the full Passive Voice.

78 THE CONJUGATIONS.

Verbs are generally arranged according to the Character of the Present Stem in four Conjugations.

The Character is most clearly seen before the suffix -re (or -ĕre) of the Infinitive Present Active. It is either one of the vowels a, e, i, u, or a **Consonant**.

First Conjugation, **A- Stems.**
Second Conjugation, **E- Stems.**
Third Conjugation, **Consonant and U- Stems.**
Fourth Conjugation, **I- Stems.**

Deponent Verbs are also divided into four Conjugations with the same Stem endings.

79 The following forms must be known in order to give the full Conjugation.

	A- Stems.	E- Stems.	Consonant and U- Stems.	I- Stems.
	Active Voice.			
1 Pers. Pres. Indic.	ămo	mŏneo	rĕgo	audĭo
Infin. Pres.	amārĕ	monērĕ	regĕrĕ	audīrĕ
Perfect.	amāvī	monuī	rexī	audīvī
Supine in -um.	amātum	monĭtum	rectum	audītum
	Passive Voice.			
1 Pers. Pres. Indic.	amor	moneor	regor	audior
Infin. Pres.	amārī	monērī	regī	audīrī
Partic. Perf.	amātus	monĭtus	rectus	audītus
Gerundive	amandus	monendus	regendus	audiendus

When the Perfect ends in -**vi**, a shortened form is often used: amavisti becomes amasti; amāvērunt, amārunt; audīvi, audii; audīvērunt, audiērunt.

For -**ērunt** (3rd pers. pl. Perf. Indic.) -**ēre** was often used amavēre, audīvēre.

The 2nd pers. sing. ends in -**ris** or -**re** in the Passive: amābāris, amābāre; but usually -**ris** in the Pres. Indic.

80 PERIPHRASTIC CONJUGATION.

The Active Future Participle and the Gerundive may be used with the Infinitive esse and with all the Tenses of the Verb sum :

amaturus, -a sum,   *I am about to love.*
amaturus, -a es,   *thou art about to love.*
amaturus, -a est,   *he (she) is about to love.*
amaturi,   -ae sumus, *we are about to love.*
    etc.
amandus, -a sum,   *I am meet to be loved.*
    etc.

In the same way the Participle futurus may be used with the tenses of sum: futurus sum, *I am about to be.*

The Active Future Participle with fuisse forms an Imperfect Future Infinitive, which is only used conditionally: amaturus fuisse, *to have been about to love.*

81

*The Verb **Sum**, I am*

TENSE.	INDICATIVE.	
Present.	sum,	I am.
	ĕs,	thou art.
	est,	he is.
	sŭmŭs,	we are.
	estĭs,	ye are.
	sunt,	they are.
Future Simple.	ĕro,	I shall be.
	erĭs,	thou wilt be.
	erĭt,	he will be.
	erĭmŭs,	we shall be.
	erĭtĭs,	ye will be.
	erunt,	they will be.
Imperfect.	eram,	I was.
	erăs,	thou wast.
	erăt,	he was.
	erămŭs,	we were.
	erătĭs,	ye were.
	erant,	they were.
Perfect.	fuī,	I have been or I was.
	fuistī,	thou hast been or thou wast.
	fuĭt,	he has been or he was.
	fuĭmŭs,	we have been or we were.
	fuistĭs,	ye have been or ye were.
	fuērunt,	they have been or they were.
Future Perfect.	fuĕro,	I shall have been.
	fuĕrĭs,	thou wilt have been.
	fuĕrĭt,	he will have been.
	fuĕrĭmŭs,	we shall have been.
	fuĕrĭtĭs,	ye will have been.
	fuĕrint,	they will have been.
Pluperfect.	fuĕram,	I had been.
	fuĕrăs,	thou hadst been.
	fuĕrăt,	he had been.
	fuĕrămŭs,	we had been.
	fuĕrătĭs,	ye had been.
	fuĕrant,	they had been.

* Before the regular Verbs it is necessary to conjugate the
as an auxiliary in the conjugation of other Verbs.

(sum, fui, esse, futurus).

SUBJUNCTIVE.	IMPERATIVE.
sim sīs sĭt sīmŭs sītĭs sint	ĕs, estō, *be thou.* estō, *let him be.* estĕ, estōtĕ, *be ye.* suntō, *let them be.*
	THE VERB INFINITE. **Infinitives.** Present Imperf. } essĕ, *to be.*
essem *or* fŏrem essēs *or* fŏrēs essĕt *or* fŏrĕt essēmŭs essētĭs essent *or* fŏrent	Perfect Pluperf. } fuissĕ, *to have been.* Future { fŭtūrŭs essĕ forĕ } *to be about to be.* **Participles.**
fuĕrim fuĕris fuĕrĭt fuĕrĭmŭs fuĕrĭtĭs fuĕrint	Present (*none*). Future fŭtūrŭs, *about to be.* **Gerunds and Supines.** (*None.*)
	Note.—There is no present participle of sum. It is only seen in the compounds, ab-sens, prae-sens.
fuissem fuissēs fuissĕt fuissēmŭs fuissētĭs fuissent	Like Sum are conjugated its compounds: absum, *am absent*; adsum, *am present*; dēsum, *am wanting*; insum, *am in* or *among*; intersum, *am among*; obsum, *hinder*; praesum, *am set over*; prōsum, *am of use*; subsum, *am under*; supersum, *survive.* In prōsum the final d of the old preposition is kept before e: prodes.

irregular Verb of Being. sum, *I am*, esse, *to be*, because it is used

TENSE.	INDICATIVE.	
Present	ămŏ,	*I love* or *am loving.*
	amās,	*thou lovest* or *art loving.*
	amăt,	*he loves* or *is loving.*
	amāmŭs,	*we love* or *are loving.*
	amātĭs,	*ye love* or *are loving.*
	amant,	*they love* or *are loving.*
Future Simple.	amābo,	*I shall love.*
	amābĭs,	*thou wilt love.*
	amābĭt,	*he will love.*
	amābĭmŭs,	*we shall love.*
	amābĭtĭs,	*ye will love.*
	amābunt,	*they will love.*
Imperfect.	amābam,	*I was loving* or *I loved.*
	amābās,	*thou wast loving* or *thou lovedst.*
	amābăt,	*he was loving* or *he loved.*
	amābāmŭs,	*we were loving* or *we loved.*
	amābātĭs,	*ye were loving* or *ye loved.*
	amābant,	*they were loving* or *they loved.*
Perfect.	amāvī,	*I have loved* or *I loved.*
	amāvistī,	*thou hast loved* or *thou lovedst.*
	amāvĭt,	*he has loved* or *he loved*
	amāvĭmŭs,	*we have loved* or *we loved.*
	amāvistĭs,	*ye have loved* or *ye loved.*
	amāvērunt,	*they have loved* or *they loved.*
Future Perfect.	amāvĕrŏ,	*I shall have loved.*
	amāvĕrĭs,	*thou wilt have loved.*
	amāvĕrĭt,	*he will have loved.*
	amāvĕrĭmŭs,	*we shall have loved.*
	amāvĕrĭtĭs,	*ye will have loved.*
	amāvĕrint,	*they will have loved.*
Pluperfect.	amāvĕram,	*I had loved.*
	amāvĕrās,	*thou hadst loved.*
	amāvĕrăt,	*he had loved.*
	amāvĕrāmŭs,	*we had loved.*
	amāvĕrātĭs,	*ye had loved.*
	amāvĕrant,	*they had loved.*

A- STEMS.

VOICE.

SUBJUNCTIVE.	IMPERATIVE.
amem amĕs amĕt amēmŭs amētĭs ament	amă, amātō, *love thou.* amātō, *let him love.* amātĕ, amātōtĕ, *love ye.* amantō, *let them love.*

THE VERB INFINITE.

Infinitives.

amārem amārēs amārĕt amārēmŭs amārētĭs amārent	Present Imperf. } amārĕ, *to love.* Perfect Pluperf. } amāvissĕ, *to have loved.* Future amātūrŭs essĕ, *to be about to love.*
amāvĕrim amāvĕris amāvĕrĭt amāvĕrimŭs amāvĕrĭtĭs amāvĕrint	<center>Gerunds.</center> Nom. Acc. amandum, *the loving.* Gen. amandī, *of loving.* Dat. Abl. amando, *for* or *by loving.*

Supines.

amātum, *in order to love.*
amātū, *in* or *for loving.*

amāvissem amāvissēs amāvissēt amāvissēmŭs amāvissētĭs amāvissent	<center>Participles.</center> Pres. amans, *loving.* Fut. amātūrŭs, *about to love.*

83

TENSE.	INDICATIVE.	
Present.	mŏneō,	*I advise* or *am advising.*
	monĕs,	*thou advisest* or *art advising.*
	monĕt,	*he advises* or *is advising.*
	monēmŭs,	*we advise* or *are advising.*
	monētĭs,	*ye advise* or *are advising.*
	monent,	*they advise* or *are advising.*
Future Simple.	monēbō,	*I shall advise.*
	monēbĭs,	*thou wilt advise.*
	monēbĭt,	*he will advise.*
	monēbĭmŭs,	*we shall advise.*
	monēbĭtĭs,	*ye will advise.*
	monēbunt,	*they will advise.*
Imperfect.	monēbam,	*I was advising* or *I advised.*
	monēbās,	*thou wast advising* or *thou advisedst.*
	monēbăt,	*he was advising* or *he advised.*
	monēbāmŭs,	*we were advising* or *we advised.*
	monēbātĭs,	*ye were advising* or *ye advised.*
	monēbant,	*they were advising* or *they advised.*
Perfect.	monuī,	*I have advised* or *I advised.*
	monuistī,	*thou hast advised* or *thou advisedst.*
	monuĭt,	*he has advised* or *he advised.*
	monuĭmŭs,	*we have advised* or *we advised.*
	monuistĭs,	*ye have advised* or *ye advised.*
	monuērunt,	*they have advised* or *they advised.*
Future Perfect.	monuĕro,	*I shall have advised.*
	monuĕrĭs,	*thou wilt have advised.*
	monuĕrĭt,	*he will have advised.*
	monuĕrĭmŭs,	*we shall have advised.*
	monuĕrĭtĭs,	*ye will have advised.*
	monuĕrint,	*they will have advised.*
Pluperfect.	monuĕram,	*I had advised.*
	monuĕrās,	*thou hadst advised.*
	monuĕrăt,	*he had advised.*
	monuĕrāmŭs,	*we had advised.*
	monuĕrātĭs,	*ye had advised.*
	monuĕrant,	*they had advised.*

E- Stems.

VOÏCE.

Subjunctive.	Imperative.
moneam moneās moneăt moneāmŭs moneātĭs moneant	monē, monētō, *advise thou.* monētō, *let him advise.* monētĕ, monētōtĕ, *advise ye.* monentō, *let them advise.*

The Verb Infinite.

Infinitives.

monērem monērēs monērĕt monērēmŭs monērētĭs monērent	Present } Imperf. } monērĕ, *to advise.* Perfect } Pluperf. } monuissĕ, *to have advised.* Future monĭtūrŭs essĕ, *to be about to advise.*

Gerunds.

Nom. Acc. monendum, *the advising.*
Gen.   monendī,   *of advising.*
Dat. Abl. monendō,   *for* or *by advising.*

| monuĕrim
monuĕrĭs
monuĕrĭt
monuĕrĭmŭs
monuĕrĭtĭs
monuĕrint | |

Supines.

monĭtum, *in order to advise.*
monĭtū,   *in* or *for advising.*

Participles.

| monuissem
monuissēs
monuissĕt
monuissēmŭs
monuissētĭs
monuissent | Pres. monens, *advising.*
Fut. monĭtūrŭs, *about to advise.* |

84   THIRD CONJUGATION

ACTIVE

		INDICATIVE.
Present.	rĕgŏ regĭs, regĭt, regĭmŭs, regĭtĭs, regunt,	*I rule* or *am ruling.* *thou rulest* or *art ruling.* *he rules* or *is ruling.* *we rule* or *are ruling.* *ye rule* or *are ruling.* *they rule* or *are ruling.*
Future Simple.	regam, regēs, regĕt, regēmŭs, regētĭs, regent,	*I shall rule.* *thou wilt rule.* *he will rule.* *we shall rule.* *ye will rule.* *they will rule.*
Imperfect.	regēbam, regēbās, regēbăt, regēbāmŭs, regēbātĭs, regēbant,	*I was ruling* or *I ruled.* *thou wast ruling* or *thou ruledst.* *he was ruling* or *he ruled.* *we were ruling* or *we ruled.* *ye were ruling* or *ye ruled.* *they were ruling* or *they ruled.*
Perfect.	rēxī, rexistī, rexĭt, rexĭmŭs, rexistĭs, rexērunt,	*I have ruled* or *I ruled.* *thou hast ruled* or *thou ruledst.* *he has ruled* or *he ruled.* *we have ruled* or *we ruled.* *ye have ruled* or *ye ruled.* *they have ruled* or *they ruled.*
Future Perfect.	rexĕrŏ, rexĕrĭs, rexĕrĭt, rexĕrĭmŭs rexĕrĭtĭs, rexĕrint,	*I shall have ruled.* *thou wilt have ruled.* *he will have ruled.* *we shall have ruled.* *ye will have ruled.* *they will have ruled.*
Pluperfect.	rexĕram, rexĕrās, rexĕrăt, rexĕrāmŭs, rexĕrātĭs, rexĕrant,	*I had ruled.* *thou hadst ruled.* *he had ruled.* *we had ruled.* *ye had ruled.* *they had ruled.*

Facio, dīco, dūco, and the compounds of duco, in the 2nd person

CONSONANT STEMS.

VOICE.

SUBJUNCTIVE.	IMPERATIVE.
regam regās regăt regāmŭs regātĭs regant	regĕ, regĭtō, *rule thou.* regĭtō, *let him rule.* regĭtĕ, regĭtōtĕ, *rule ye.* reguntō, *let them rule.*

THE VERB INFINITE.

Infinitives.

| regĕrem
regĕrēs
regĕrĕt
regĕrēmŭs
regĕrētĭs
regĕrent | Present } Imperf.} regĕrĕ, *to rule,* |

Perfect } Pluperf.} rexissĕ, *to have ruled.*

| rexĕrim
rexĕrīs
rexĕrĭt
rexĕrĭmŭs
rexĕrĭtĭs
rexĕrint | Future   rectūrŭs essĕ, *to be about to rule.* |

Gerunds.

Nom. Acc. regendum, *the ruling*
Gen.   regendī,   *of ruling.*
Dat. Abl. regendō,   *for* or *by ruling.*

Supines.

rectum, *in order to rule.*
rectū,   *in* or *for ruling.*

| rexissem
rexissēs
rexissĕt
rexissēmŭs
rexissētĭs
rexissent | Participles. |

Present   regens, *ruling.*
Future   rectūrŭs, *about to rule.*

of the Pres. Imperative make făc, dīc. dūc. &c.

TENSE.	INDICATIVE.	
Present.	audĭŏ,	*I hear* or *am hearing.*
	audīs,	*thou hearest* or *art hearing.*
	audĭt,	*he hears* or *is hearing.*
	audīmŭs,	*we hear* or *are hearing.*
	audītĭs,	*ye hear* or *are hearing.*
	audĭunt,	*they hear* or *are hearing.*
Future Simple.	audĭam,	*I shall hear*
	audĭēs,	*thou wilt hear.*
	audĭēt,	*he will hear.*
	audĭēmŭs,	*we shall hear.*
	audĭētĭs,	*ye will hear.*
	audĭent,	*they will hear.*
Imperfect.	audĭēbam,	*I was hearing* or *I heard.*
	audĭēbās,	*thou wast hearing* or *heardest.*
	audĭēbăt,	*he was hearing* or *he heard.*
	audĭēbāmŭs,	*we were hearing* or *we heard.*
	audĭēbātĭs,	*ye were hearing* or *ye heard.*
	audĭēbant,	*they were hearing* or *they heard.*
Perfect.	audīvī,	*I have heard* or *I heard.*
	audīvistī,	*thou hast heard* or *thou heardest.*
	audīvĭt,	*he has heard* or *he heard.*
	audīvĭmŭs,	*we have heard* or *we heard.*
	audīvistĭs,	*ye have heard* or *ye heard.*
	audīvērunt,	*they have heard* or *they heard.*
Future Perfect.	audīvĕro,	*I shall have heard.*
	audīvĕrĭs,	*thou wilt have heard.*
	audīvĕrĭt,	*he will have heard.*
	audīvĕrĭmŭs,	*we shall have heard.*
	audīvĕritĭs,	*ye will have heard.*
	audīvĕrint,	*they will have heard.*
Pluperfect.	audīvĕram,	*I had heard.*
	audīvĕrās,	*thou hadst heard.*
	audīvĕrăt,	*he had heard.*
	audīvĕrāmŭs,	*we had heard.*
	audīvĕrātĭs,	*ye had heard.*
	audīvĕrant,	*they had heard.*

I- Stems.

VOICE.

Subjunctive.	Imperative.
audĭam audĭās audĭăt audĭāmŭs audĭātĭs audĭant	audī, audītō, *hear thou.* audītō, *let him hear.* audĭtĕ, audītōtĕ, *hear ye.* audiuntō, *let them hear.*

The Verb Infinite.

Infinitives.

audīrem audīrēs audīrĕt audīrēmŭs audīrētĭs audīrent	Present Imperf. } audīre, *to hear.*

Perfect Pluperf. } audīvissĕ, *to have heard.*

Future   audītūrŭs essĕ, *to be about to hear.*

Gerunds.

audīvĕrim audīvĕrĭs audīvĕrĭt audīvĕrĭmŭs audīvĕrĭtĭs audīvĕrint	Nom. Acc. audĭ ndum, *the hearing.*

Nom. Acc.   audĭ ndum, *the hearing.*
Gen.   audiendī,   *of hearing.*
Dat. Abl.   audiendō,   *for* or *by hearing.*

Supines.

audītum, *in order to hear.*
audītū,   *in* or *for hearing.*

Participles.

audīvissem audīvissēs audīvissĕt audīvissēmŭs audīvissētĭs audīvissent	Present audiens, *hearing.* Future audītūrŭs, *about to hear.*

Tense.	Indicative.	
Present.	ămor,	*I am* or *I am being loved.*
	amāris,	*thou art* or *thou art being loved.*
	amātŭr,	*he is* or *he is being loved.*
	amāmŭr,	*we are* or *we are being loved.*
	amāmĭnī,	*ye are* or *ye are being loved.*
	amantŭr,	*they are* or *they are being loved.*
Future Simple.	amābŏr,	*I shall be loved.*
	amābĕris,	*thou wilt be loved.*
	amābĭtŭr,	*he will be loved.*
	amābĭmŭr,	*we shall be loved.*
	amābĭmĭnī,	*ye will be loved.*
	amābuntŭr,	*they will be loved.*
Imperfect.	amābăr,	*I was being* or *I was loved.*
	amābāris,	*thou wast being* or *thou wast loved.*
	amābātŭr,	*he was being* or *he was loved.*
	amābāmŭr,	*we were being* or *we were loved.*
	amābāmĭnī,	*ye were being* or *ye were loved.*
	amābantŭr,	*they were being* or *they were loved.*
Perfect.	amātŭs sum,	*I have been* or *I was loved.*
	amātŭs ĕs,	*thou hast been* or *thou wast loved.*
	amātŭs est,	*he has been* or *he was loved.*
	amātī sŭmŭs,	*we have been* or *we were loved.*
	amātī estĭs,	*ye have been* or *ye were loved.*
	amātī sunt,	*they have been* or *they were loved.*
Future Perfect.	amātŭs ĕrō,	*I shall have been loved.*
	amātŭs ĕrĭs,	*thou wilt have been loved.*
	amātŭs ĕrĭt,	*he will have been loved.*
	amātī ĕrĭmŭs,	*we shall have been loved.*
	amātī ĕrĭtĭs,	*ye will have been loved.*
	amātī ĕrunt,	*they will have been loved.*
Pluperfect.	amātŭs ĕram,	*I had been loved.*
	amātŭs ĕrās,	*thou hadst been loved.*
	amātus ĕrăt,	*he had been loved.*
	amātī ĕrāmŭs,	*we had been loved.*
	amātī ĕrātĭs,	*ye had been loved.*
	amātī ĕrant,	*they had been loved.*

A- STEMS.

VOICE.

SUBJUNCTIVE.	IMPERATIVE.
amĕr amēris amētŭr amēmŭr amēmĭnī amentŭr	amārĕ, amātŏr, *be thou loved.* amātŏr, *let him be loved.* amāmĭnī, *be ye loved.* amantŏr, *let them be loved.*
amārĕr amārēris amārētŭr amārēmŭr amārēmĭnī amārentŭr	**THE VERB INFINITE.** Infinitives.
amātŭs sim amātŭs sīs amātŭs sĭt amātī sīmus amātī sītis amātī sint	Present Imperf.} amārī, *to be loved.* Perfect Pluperf.} amātŭs essĕ, *to have been loved.* Future amātum īrī (225).
	Participle. Perfect amātŭs, *loved,* or *having been loved.*
amātŭs essem amātŭs essēs amātŭs essĕt amātī essēmŭs amātī essētĭs amātī essent	Gerundive. amandŭs, *meet to be loved.*

        SECOND CONJUGATION

PASSIVE

TENSE.	INDICATIVE.	
Present.	mŏnĕŏr,	*I am* or *I am being advised.*
	monērĭs,	*thou art* or *thou art being advised.*
	monētŭr,	*he is* or *he is being advised.*
	monēmŭr,	*we are* or *we are being advised.*
	monēmĭnī	*ye are* or *ye are being advised.*
	monentŭr,	*they are* or *they are being advised.*
Future Simple.	monēbŏr,	*I shall be advised.*
	monēbĕrĭs,	*thou wilt be advised.*
	monēbĭtŭr,	*he will be advised.*
	monēbĭmŭr,	*we shall be advised.*
	monēbĭmĭnī,	*ye will be advised.*
	monēbuntŭr,	*they will be advised.*
Imperf.	monēbăr,	*I was being* or *I was advised.*
	monēbārĭs,	*thou wast being* or *thou wast advised.*
	monēbātŭr,	*he was being* or *he was advised.*
	monēbāmŭr,	*we were being* or *we were advised.*
	monēbāmĭnī,	*ye were being* or *ye were advised.*
	monēbantŭr,	*they were being* or *they were advised.*
Perfect.	monĭtŭs sum	*I have been* or *I was advised.*
	monĭtŭs ĕs,	*thou hast been* or *thou wast advised.*
	monĭtŭs est,	*he has been* or *he was advised.*
	monĭtī sŭmŭs,	*we have been* or *we were advised.*
	monĭtī estĭs,	*ye have been* or *ye were advised.*
	monĭtī sunt,	*they have been* or *they were advised.*
Future Perfect.	monĭtŭs ĕrō,	*I shall have been advised.*
	monĭtŭs ĕrĭs,	*thou wilt have been advised.*
	monĭtŭs ĕrĭt,	*he will have been advised.*
	monĭtī ĕrĭmŭs,	*we shall have been advised.*
	monĭtī ĕrĭtĭs,	*ye will have been advised.*
	monĭtī ĕrunt,	*they will have been advised.*
Pluperf.	monĭtŭs ĕram,	*I had been advised.*
	monĭtŭs ĕrās,	*thou hadst been advised.*
	monĭtŭs ĕrăt,	*he had been advised.*
	monĭtī ĕrāmus,	*we had been advised.*
	monĭtī ĕrātĭs,	*ye had been advised.*
	monĭtī ĕrant,	*they had been advised.*

E- Stems.

VOICE.

Subjunctive.	Imperative.
monĕăr monĕārĭs monĕātŭr monĕāmŭr monĕāmĭnī monĕantŭr	monērĕ, monētŏr, *be thou advised.* monētŏr, *let him be advised.* monēmĭnī, *be ye advised.* monentŏr, *let them be advised.*
monērĕr monērērĭs monērētŭr monērēmŭr monērēmĭnī monērentŭr	**The Verb Infinite.** Infinitives.
monĭtŭs sim monĭtŭs sīs monĭtŭs sĭt monĭti sĭmus monĭti sītis monĭti sint	Present Imperf. } monērī, *to be advised.* Perfect Pluperf. } monĭtŭs essĕ, *to have been advised.* Future monĭtum īrī (225). Participle. Perfect monĭtŭs, *advised,* or *having been advised.* Gerundive.
monĭtŭs essem monĭtŭs essēs monĭtŭs essĕt monĭti essēmŭs monĭti essētĭs monĭti essent	monendŭs, *meet to be advised.*

88   Tʜɪʀᴅ Cᴏɴᴊᴜɢᴀᴛɪᴏɴ

PASSIVE

Tᴇɴsᴇ.	Iɴᴅɪᴄᴀᴛɪᴠᴇ.	
Present.	rĕgŏr,	*I am* or *I am being ruled.*
	regĕrĭs,	*thou art* or *thou art being ruled.*
	regĭtŭr,	*he is* or *he is being ruled.*
	regĭmŭr,	*wĕ are* or *we are being ruled.*
	regĭmĭnĭ,	*ye are* or *ye are being ruled.*
	reguntŭr,	*they are* or *they are being ruled.*
Future Simple.	regăr,	*I shall be ruled.*
	regērĭs,	*thou wilt be ruled.*
	regētŭr,	*he will be ruled.*
	regēmŭr,	*we shall be ruled.*
	regēmĭnĭ,	*ye will be ruled.*
	regentŭr,	*they will be ruled.*
Imperfect.	regēbăr,	*I was being* or *I was ruled.*
	regēbārĭs,	*thou wast being* or *thou wast ruled.*
	regēbātŭr,	*he was being* or *he was ruled.*
	regēbāmŭr,	*we were being* or *we were ruled.*
	regēbāmĭnĭ,	*ye were being* or *ye were ruled.*
	regēbantŭr,	*they were being* or *they were ruled.*
Perfect.	rectŭs sum,	*I have been* or *I was ruled.*
	rectŭs ĕs,	*thou hast been* or *thou wast ruled.*
	rectŭs est,	*he has been* or *he was ruled.*
	rectī sŭmŭs,	*we have been* or *we were ruled.*
	rectī estĭs,	*ye have been* or *ye were ruled.*
	rectī sunt,	*they have been* or *they were ruled.*
Future Perfect.	rectŭs ĕrō,	*I shall have been ruled.*
	rectŭs ĕrĭs,	*thou wilt have been ruled.*
	rectŭs ĕrĭt,	*he will have been ruled.*
	rectī ĕrĭmŭs,	*we shall have been ruled.*
	rectī erĭtĭs,	*ye will have been ruled.*
	rectī ĕrunt,	*they will have been ruled.*
Pluperfect.	rectŭs ĕram,	*I had been ruled.*
	rectŭs ĕrās,	*thou hadst been ruled.*
	rectŭs ĕrăt,	*he had been ruled.*
	rectī ĕrāmŭs,	*we had been ruled.*
	rectī ĕrātĭs,	*ye had been ruled.*
	rectī ĕrant,	*they had been ruled.*

CONSONANT STEMS.

VOICE.

SUBJUNCTIVE.	IMPERATIVE.
regăr regārĭs regātŭr regāmŭr regāmĭnī regantŭr	regĕrĕ, regĭtŏr, *be thou ruled.* regĭtŏr, *let him be ruled.* regĭmĭnī, *be ye ruled.* reguntŏr, *let them be ruled.*
regĕrĕr regĕrērĭs regĕrētŭr regĕrēmŭr regĕrēmĭnī regĕrentŭr	
rectŭs sim rectŭs sīs rectŭs sĭt rectī sīmŭs rectī sītĭs rectī sint	'THE VERB INFINITE. Infinitives. Present } Imperf. } rĕgī, *to be ruled.* Perfect } Pluperf. } rectŭs essĕ, *to have been ruled.* Future rectum īrī (225). Participle. Perfect rectŭs, *ruled,* or *having been ruled.* Gerundive. rĕgendŭs, *meet to be ruled.*
rectŭs essem rectŭs essēs rectŭs essĕt rectī essēmŭs rectī essētĭs rectī essent	

TENSE.	INDICATIVE.	
Present.	audĭŏr,	I am or I am being heard.
	audīrĭs,	thou art or thou art being heard.
	audītŭr,	he is or he is being heard.
	audīmŭr,	we are or we are being heard.
	audīmĭnī,	ye are or ye are being heard.
	audiuntŭr,	they are or they are being heard.
Future Simple.	audiăr,	I shall be heard.
	audiērĭs,	thou wilt be heard.
	audiētŭr,	he will be heard.
	audiēmŭr,	we shall be heard.
	audiēmĭnī,	ye will be heard.
	audientŭr,	they will be heard.
Imperf.	audiēbăr,	I was being or I was heard.
	audiēbārĭs,	thou wast being or thou wast heard
	audiēbātŭr,	he was being or he was heard.
	audiēbāmŭr,	we were being or we were heard.
	audiēbāmĭnī,	ye were being or ye were heard.
	audiēbāntŭr,	they were being or they were heard.
Perfect.	audītŭs sum,	I have been or I was heard.
	audītŭs ĕs,	thou hast been or thou wast heard.
	audītŭs est,	he has been or he was heard.
	audītī sŭmŭs,	we have been or we were heard.
	audītī estĭs,	ye have been or ye were heard.
	audītī sunt,	they have been or they were heard.
Future Perfect.	audītŭs ĕrō,	I shall have been heard.
	audītŭs ĕrĭs,	thou wilt have been heard.
	audītŭs ĕrĭt,	he will have been heard.
	audītī ĕrĭmŭs,	we shall have been heard.
	audītī ĕrĭtĭs,	ye will have been heard.
	audītī ĕrunt,	they will have been heard.
Pluperf.	audītŭs ĕram,	I had been heard.
	audītŭs ĕrās,	thou hadst been heard.
	audītŭs ĕrăt,	he had been heard.
	audītī ĕrāmŭs,	we had been heard.
	audītī ĕrātĭs,	ye had been heard.
	audītī ĕrant,	they had been heard.

I-STEMS.

VOICE.

SUBJUNCTIVE.	IMPERATIVE.
audiăr audiārĭs audiātŭr audiāmŭr audiāmĭnĭ audiantŭr	audīrĕ, audītŏr, *be thou heard.* audītŏr, *let him be heard.* audīmĭnĭ, *be ye heard.* audiuntŏr, *let them be heard.*
audīrĕr audīrērĭs audīrētŭr audīrēmŭr audīrēmĭnĭ audīrentŭr	**THE VERB INFINITE.** **Infinitives.**
audītŭs sim audītŭs sīs audītŭs sĭt audītī sīmŭs audītī sītĭs audītī sint	Present } Imperf. } audīrī, *to be heard.* Perfect } Pluperf. } audītŭs essĕ, *to have been heard.* Future audītum īrī (225). **Participle.** Perfect audītŭs, *heard,* or *having been heard.*
audītŭs essem audītŭs essēs audītŭs essĕt audītī essēmŭs audītī essētĭs audītī essent	**Gerundive.** audiendŭs, *meet to be heard.*

90   Ūtor, ūti, ūsus, *use*

DEPONENT VERB, HAVING THE FORMS OF THE PASSIVE

TENSE.	INDICATIVE.	
Present.	ūtŏr,	I use.
	utĕris,	thou usest.
	utĭtŭr,	he uses.
	utĭmŭr,	we use.
	utĭmĭni,	ye use.
	utuntŭr,	they use.
Future Simple.	utăr,	I shall use.
	utēris,	thou wilt use.
	utētŭr,	he will use.
	utēmŭr,	we shall use.
	utēmĭnī,	ye will use.
	utentŭr,	they will use.
Imperfect.	utēbăr,	I was using or I used.
	utēbāris.	thou wast using or thou didst use.
	utēbātŭr,	he was using or he used.
	utēbāmŭr,	we were using or we used.
	utēbāmĭnī,	ye were using or ye used.
	utēbantŭr,	they were using or they used.
Perfect.	ūsŭs sum,	I have used or I used.
	usŭs es,	thou hast used or thou didst use.
	ūsŭs est,	he has used or he used.
	usī sumŭs,	we have used or we used.
	usī estis,	ye have used or ye used.
	usī sunt,	they have used or they used.
Future Perfect.	usŭs ĕrŏ,	I shall have used.
	usŭs ĕris,	thou wilt have used.
	usŭs ĕrĭt,	he will have used.
	usī ĕrimŭs,	we shall have used.
	usī ĕrĭtis,	ye will have used.
	usī ĕrunt,	they will have used.
Pluperfect.	usŭs ĕram,	I had used.
	usŭs ĕrās,	thou hadst used.
	usŭs ĕrăt,	he had used.
	usī ĕrāmŭs,	we had used.
	usī ĕrātĭs,	ye had used.
	usī ĕrant,	they had used.

Deponent Verbs have Gerunds, Supines, Present and Future Participle

(Third Conjugation).

Voice, with the Meaning of the Active.

Subjunctive.	Imperative.
ūtăr utārĭs utātŭr utāmŭr utāmĭnī utantŭr	utĕrĕ, utĭtŏr, *use thou.* utĭtŏr, *let him use.* utĭmĭnī, *use ye.* utuntŏr, *let them use.*

The Verb Infinite.

Infinitives.

Present Imperf. }	utī, *to use.*
Perfect Pluperf. }	usŭs esse, *to have used.*
Future	usūrŭs essĕ, *to be about to use.*

utĕrĕr
utĕrērĭs
utĕrētŭr
utĕrēmŭr
utĕrēmĭnī
utĕrentŭr

Gerunds.

Nom. Acc.	utendum,	*using.*
Gen.	utendī,	*of using.*
Dat. Abl.	utendō,	*for* or *by using.*

usŭs sim
usŭs sīs
usŭs sĭt
usī sīmŭs
usī sĭtĭs
usī sint

Supines.

usum, *to use.*

usū, *in* or *for using.*

Participles.

Present	utens,	*using.*
Future	usūrŭs,	*about to use.*
Perfect	usŭs,	*having used.*

usŭs essem
usŭs essēs
usŭs essĕt
usī essēmŭs
usī essētĭs
usī essent

Gerundive.

utendŭs, *meet to be used.*

Active; their Perfect Participles have the meaning of the Active Voice.

91   Many Perf. Participles of Deponent Verbs are used passively as well as actively: as confessus from confíteor, *confess*; imitātus from imitor, *imitate*; měrítus from měreor, *deserve*; pollĭcĭtus from pollĭceor, *promise*.

92   Some Verbs have a Perfect of Passive form with a Present of Active form; they are called **Semi-deponents**:

audeo, *dare*   ausus sum, *I have dared or I dared.*
gaudeo, *rejoice*   gāvīsus sum, *I have rejoiced or I rejoiced.*
sŏleo, *am wont*   solītus sum, *I have been wont or I was wont.*
fīdo, *trust*   fīsus sum, *I have trusted or I trusted.*

93   Some Verbs have an Active form with Passive meaning; they are called Quasi-Passive:

exŭlo,   *am banished.*   lĭceo,   *am put up for sale.*
vāpŭlo,   *am beaten.*   vēneo,   *am on sale.*
fĭo,   *am made.*

94   Some Verbs have Perfect Participles with Active meaning like the Deponent Verbs:

jūro,   *swear.*   jurāvi,   *I swore.*   jurātus, *having sworn.*
cēno,   *sup.*   cenāvi,   *I supped.*   cenātus, *having supped.*
prandeo, *dine.*   prandi,   *I dined.*   pransus, *having dined.*

95   **Inceptive** Verbs, with Present Stem in -**sco** (Third Conjugation), express beginning of action, and are derived from Verb-Stems or from Nouns:

pallesco,   *turn pale,*   from palleo.
nigresco,   *turn black,*   from niger.

96   **Frequentative** Verbs (First Conj.) express repeated or intenser action, and are formed from Supine Stems:

rŏgito, *ask repeatedly* (rogo); canto, *sing with energy* (căno).

97   **Desiderative** Verbs (Fourth Conj.) express desire of action, and are formed from the Supine Stem:

ēsŭrio, *am hungry* (ĕdō, ēsurus).

98

VERBS IN -io (THIRD CONJUGATION).

Forms from Present Stem, cap-i-, *take*.

		ACTIVE VOICE				PASSIVE VOICE	
		INDIC.	SUBJUNC.			INDIC.	SUBJUNC.
Present		căpio capis capit capĭmus capitis capiunt	capiam capias capiat capiamus capiatis capiant	Present		capior capĕris capĭtur capimur capimini capiuntur	capiar capiaris capiatur capiamur capiamini capiantur
Fut. Simple		capiam capies capiet capiēmus capietis capient		Fut. Simple		capiar capiĕris capietur capiemur capiemini capientur	
Imperf.		capiēbam capiebas capiebat capiebamus capiebatis capiebant	capĕrem caperes caperet caperemus caperetis caperent	Imperf.		capiēbar capiebaris capiebatur capiebamur capiebamini capiebantur	capĕrer capereris caperetur caperemur caperemini caperentur
Imperative	Sing	2. cape, capito. 3. capito.			2. capĕre, capitor. 3. capitor.		
	Plur.	2. capite, capitōte. 3. capiunto.			2. capĭmini. 3. capiuntor.		
		Infin. Pres. căpĕre. Gerund. capiendum. Pres. Partic. capiens.				Infin. Pres. capi. Gerundive capiendus.	

Capio has Perfect cēpi ; Supine captum.

The Verbs in -io are :

căpio, cŭpio *and* făcio, fŏdio, fŭgio *and* jăcio, părio, răpio, săpio, quătio, } *and their* compounds,	take, desire, make, dig, fly, throw, bring forth, seize, know, shake,
Compounds of spĕcio *and* lăcio { obsolete Verbs,	look at, entice,
Deponent : grădior, pătior, mŏrior, And in some tenses, pŏtior, ŏrior,	step, suffer, die, get possession of, arise.

99   IRREGULAR VERBS.

Verbs are called irregular :

(1) Because they are formed from more than one root,
as sum.

(2) Because their tense-forms differ from those of regular
verbs.

100   Possum, *I can*, potui, posse.

The Pres. Indic. possum is compounded of sum, *I am*, and
the adjective potis *or* poti, *able*.

	INDIC.	SUBJUNC.		INDIC.	SUBJUNC.
Present	possum pŏtĕs potest possŭmus potestis possunt	possim possis possit possīmus possītis possint	**Perfect**	potui potuisti potuit potuimus potuistis potuĕrunt	potuerim potueris potuerit potuerimus potueritis potuerint
Fut. Simp.	potero poteris poterit poterĭmus poterĭtis potĕrunt		**Fut. Perf.**	potuero potueris potuerit potuerimus potueritis potuerint	
Imperf.	poteram poteras poterat poteramus poteratis poterant	possem posses posset possemus possetis possent	**Pluperf.**	potueram potueras potuerat potueramus potueratis potuerant	potuissem potuisses potuisset potuissemus potuissetis potuissent

Infinitive Pres. and Imperf. posse (pot-esse). Perf. and
Pluperf. potuisse.

Potens is used as an Adjective, *powerful, able,* never as a Participle.

101   Fĕro, *bear*, ferre, tŭli, lātum.

		ACTIVE VOICE			PASSIVE VOICE	
		INDIC.	SUBJUNC.		INDIC.	SUBJUNC.
Present		fĕro fers fert ferĭmus fertis ferunt	feram feras ferat ferāmus ferātis ferant	Present	feror ferris fertur ferĭmur ferĭmini feruntur	ferar ferāris feratur feramur feramini ferantur
Fut. Simple		feram feres feret ferēmus ferētis ferent		Fut. Simple	ferar ferēris feretur feremur feremini ferentur	
Imperf.		ferēbam ferebas ferebat ferebamus ferebatis ferebant	ferrem ferrēs ferret ferrēmus ferrētis ferrent	Imperf.	ferēbar ferebāris ferebatur ferebamur ferebamini ferebantur	ferrer ferrēris ferretur ferremur ferremini ferrentur
Imperative	Sing.	2. fer, ferto. 3. ferto.			2. ferre, fertor. 3. fertor.	
	Plur.	2. ferte, fertote. 3. ferunto.			2. ferimini. 3. feruntor.	
Infin. Pres. ferre. Gerund. ferend-um, -i, -o. Pres. Partic. ferens.				Infin. Pres. ferri. Gerundive ferendus.		

The Perfect-Stem forms are regular:

tul-i   -ero   -eram   -erim   -issem.   Infin. tulisse

Also the Supine-Stem forms:

Supines $\begin{cases} \text{latum} \\ \text{latu} \end{cases}$ Participles $\begin{cases} \text{latus} \\ \text{laturus} \end{cases}$ Infin. $\begin{cases} \text{latus e·se} \\ \text{latum iri} \end{cases}$

latus sum, ero, eram, sim, essem.

102   **Eo,** *go,* **īre, īvi or ii, ĭtum.**

	Indic.	Subjunc.	Imperative
Present	eo īs ĭt īmus ītis eunt	eam eas eat eāmus eātis eant	ī, īto. īto. īte, ītōte. eunto.
Fut. Simple	ībo ībis ībit ībimus ībitis ībunt		**The Verb Infinitive.** Infinitives. Present } īre. Imperf. } Perfect } isse, īvisse. Pluperf. }
Imperf.	ībam ības ībat ībamus ībatis ībant	īrem īres īret īrēmus īretis īrent	Future ĭturus esse. Gerunds. Nom. Acc. eundum. Gen. eundi. Dat. Abl. eundo.
Perf.	ii or īvi iisti, ivisti iit, ivit iimus, ivĭmus iistis, ivistis iērunt, ivērunt	ĭerim ieris ierit ierĭmus ieritis ierint	Supines. ĭtum. ĭtu. Participles. Pres. ĭens (Acc. euntem). Future ĭturus.

In the Perfect Tense of **eo** the forms **ii, iisti** &c. are more usual than **īvi** &c.; also in the compounds **redii, rediisti, redisti.**

The Impersonal Passive, **ītur, ĭtum est,** is often used.

103   **Queo,** *can,* **nequeo,** *cannot,* are conjugated like **eo** in the forms which are found, but many are wanting; they have no Imperative and no Gerunds.

Ambio, *go round, canvass,* is conjugated like **audio.**

104

Vŏlo, *am willing, wish.*

Nōlo, *am unwilling, do not wish.*

Mālo, *prefer, wish rather.*

	INDICATIVE			IMPERATIVE
Present	vŏlo vīs vult volŭmus vultis volunt	nōlo nonvis nonvult nolŭmus nonvultis nolunt	mālo mavis mavult malŭmus mavultis malunt	nolī, nolīto nolīto nolīte nolitōte, nolunto Volo and malo have no Imperative.
Fut. Simple	vŏlam volēs volet volēmus volētis volent	(nōlam) noles nolet nolēmus nolētis nolent	(mālam) males malet malēmus malētis malent	THE VERB INFINITE. Infinitive.
Imperf.	volēbam volebas &c.	nolēbam nolebas &c.	malēbam malebas &c.	Present $\left\{\begin{array}{l}\text{velle}\\ \text{nolle}\\ \text{malle}\end{array}\right.$ Imperfect
	SUBJUNCTIVE			
Present	vĕlim velis velit velīmus velītis velint	nōlim nolis nolit nolīmus nolītis nolint	mālim malis malit malīmus malītis malint	Gerunds. volendum, -i, -o nolendum, -i, -o malendum, -i, -o Supines. None.
Imperf.	vellem velles vellet vellemus velletis vellent	nollem nolles nollet nollemus nelletis nollent	mallem malles mallet mallemus malletis mallent	Participles. $\left\{\begin{array}{l}\text{vŏlens}\\ \text{nōlens}\\ \text{—}\end{array}\right.$

The Perfect-Stem forms are regular :

Vŏlŭ-i	-ero	-eram	-erim	-issem	
Nōlŭ-i	-ero	-eram	-erim	-issem	Infin. $\left\{\begin{array}{l}\text{vŏluisse}\\ \text{nōluisse}\\ \text{māluisse}\end{array}\right.$
Mālŭ-i	-ero	-eram	-erim	-issem	

105 Fīo, *am made, become,* fieri, factus sum.

The Present-Stem tenses of **fio** supply a Passive to the Active verb **facio**, *make*. The Perfect tenses are borrowed from the Perfect Passive of facio formed from the Supine-Stem **facto-**.

		INDIC.	SUBJUNC.	IMPERATIVE
	Present	fīo fīs fĭt (fimus) (fitis) fiunt	fīam fias fiat fiamus fiatis fiant	fī fīte
	Fut. Simple	fīam fies fiet fiemus fietis fient		THE VERB INFINITE. Infinitives. Present } Imperf. } fĭeri Perfect } Pluperf. } factus esse.
	Imperf.	fīebam fiebas fiebat fiebamus fiebatis fiebant	fĭerem fieres fieret fieremus fieretis fierent	Future factum iri. Participle. Perfect factus. Gerundive. faciendus.
	Perf.	factus sum, &c.	factus sim, &c.	

106

DEFECTIVE VERBS.

Defective Verbs are those of which only some forms are used.

Coepi, *begin* ⎫ have only Perfect-Stem forms; but the
Memĭni, *remember* ⎬ Perfect forms are used with **Present**
Odi, *hate* ⎭ meaning.

Indicative.

Perfect.	**coepi,** *I begin.*	**memini,** *I remember.*	**ōdi,** *I hate.*
Fut. Perf.	**coepero,** *I shall begin.*	**meminero,** *I shall remember.*	**odero,** *I shall hate.*
Pluperf.	**coeperam,** *I began.*	**memineram,** *I remembered.*	**oderam,** *I hated.*

Subjunctive.

Perfect.	**coeperim**	**meminerim**	**oderim**
Pluperf.	**coepissem**	**meminissem**	**odissem**
Infin.	**coepisse,** *to begin.*	**meminisse**	**odisse**
Fut. Part.	**coeptūrus,** *about to begin.*	—	**osurus,** *about to hate.*

Coepi has a participle **coeptus**. **Odi** sometimes has **osus sum**
Memini has Imperative **memento**, Plur. **mementote**.

Nōvi (Perf. of nosco) is used with Present meaning, *I know.*

novero, ⎰**noveram**⎱ **noverim** ⎰**novissem**⎱ **Infin.** ⎰**novisse**⎱
⎱**noram**⎰ ⎱**nossem**⎰ ⎱**nosse**⎰

Aio, *I say* or *affirm.*

Ind. Pres. aio, ais, ait, —— aiunt.
Imperf. aiebam, aiebas, aiebat, aiebamus, aiebatis, aiebant
Subj. Pres. — — aiat, — — aiant
Participle. aiens

Inquam, *I say.*

Ind. Pres. inquam, inquis, inquit, inquĭmus, inquĭtĭs, inquiunt
Imperf. — — inquiebat — — inquiebant
Fut. Simple. — inquies, inquiet
Perf. inquisti, inquit
Imper. inque — inquĭto

107 IMPERSONAL VERBS.

Impersonal Verbs are used only in the forms of the Third Person Singular of each tense. The principal are the following:

Present.		Perfect.	Infinitive.
misĕret,	*it moves to pity.*	(miseruit)	(miserēre)
piget,	*it vexes.*	piguit	pigēre
paenĭtet,	*it repents.*	paenituit	paenitēre
pudet,	*it shames.*	puduit	pudēre
taedet,	*it wearies.*	taeduit	taedēre
dĕcet,	*it is becoming.*	decuit	decēre
dēdecet,	*it is unbecoming.*	dedecuit	dedecēre
libet,	*it pleases.*	libuit	libēre
licet,	*it is lawful.*	licuit	licēre
oportet,	*it behoves.*	oportuit	oportēre

108 Some Impersonals express change of weather and time:

fulgurat,	*it lightens.*	tonat,	*it thunders.*
ningit,	*it snows.*	lucescit,	*it dawns.*
pluit,	*it rains.*	vesperascit,	*it grows late.*

Interest, *it concerns* (intersum), **rēfert,** *it matters* (refero), are used impersonally **(190–193).**

109 TABLE OF VERB PERFECTS AND SUPINES.

I. A- Stems.

Present	Infin.	Perfect	Supine	
		Usual Form.		
-ō(-a-io)	-ārĕ	-āvi	-ā-tum	
amō	amārĕ	amāvi	amātum	

Exceptions.

		-ui	-itum	
sŏno	-āre	sonui	sonitum	*sound*
vĕto	-āre	vetui	vetitum	*forbid*
sĕco	-āre	secui	sectum	*cut*
		Reduplicated	-tum	
dŏ	-āre	dĕdī	dătum	*give*
stŏ	-āre	stĕti	stătum	*stand*
		-i	-tum	
jŭvo	-āre	jūv·i	jūtum	*help*

110

II. E- Stems.

		Usual Form.		
-ĕō (-e-io)	-ērĕ	-ŭī	-ĭtum	
mŏnĕō	monēre	mŏnŭī	monĭtum	

Exceptions.

		-ui	-tum	
dŏceo	-ēre	docui	doctum	*teach*
tĕneo	-ēre	tenui	tentum	*hold*
		-vi	-tum	
fleo	-ēre	flevi	flētum	*weep*
		-sĭ	-tum	
augeo	-ēre	auxi	auctum	*increase* (**tr.**)
fulgeo	-ēre	fulsi	—	*shine*
		-si	-sum	
ardeo	-ēre	arsi		*burn* (*intr.*)
haereo	-ēre	haesi	—	*stick*
jŭbeo	-ēre	jussi	jussum	*command*
măneo	-ēre	mansi	mansum	*remain*
rīdeo	-ēre	risi	risum	*laugh*
suādeo	-ēre	suasi	suasum	*advise*
		-i	-tum	
căveo	-ēre	cāv-i	cautum	*beware*
fŏveo	-ēre	fŏv-i	fotum	*cherish*
mŏveo	-ēre	mŏv-i	motum	*move* (**tr.**)

Present	*Infin.*	*Perfect*	*Supine*	
		Reduplicated	**-sum**	
pendeo	-ēre	pĕpendi	pensum	*hang* (intr.)
mordeo	-ēre	mŏmordi	morsum	*bite*
		-i	**-sum**	
sĕdeo	-ēre	sēdi	sessum	*sit*
vĭdeo	-ēre	vīdi	vīsum	*see*

111   III. Consonant and U- Stems.

Consonant Stems.

rĕgo	rĕgĕre	rexī	rectum	
		-si	**-tum**	
dīco	-ēre	dixi	dictum	*say*
dūco	-ēre	duxi	ductum	*lead*
intellĕgo	-ēre	intellexi	intellectum	*understand*
surgo	-ēre	surrexi	surrectum	*arise*
tĕgo	-ēre	texi	tectum	*cover*
trăho	-ēre	traxi	tractum	*draw*
vĕho	-ēre	vexi	vectum	*carry*
vīvo	-ēre	vixi	victum	*live*
struo	-ēre	struxi	structum	*build*
nūbo	-ēre	nupsi	nuptum	*marry*
scrībo	-ēre	scripsi	scriptum	*write*
gĕro	-ēre	gessi	gestum	*carry on*
sūmo	-ēre	sumpsi	sumptum	*take*
cingo	-ēre	cinxi	cinctum	*surround*
fingo	-ēre	finxi	fictum	*feign*
jungo	-ēre	junxi	junctum	*join*
		-si	**-sum**	
fīgo	-ēre	fixi	fixum	*fix*
spargo	-ēre	sparsi	sparsum	*sprinkle*
cēdo	-ēre	cessi	cessum	*yield*
claudo	-ēre	clausi	clausum	*shut*
dīvĭdo	-ēre	divīsi	divīsum	*divide*
lūdo	-ēre	lusi	lusum	*play*
mitto	-ēre	mīsi	missum	*send*
prĕmo	-ēre	pressi	pressum	*press*
concŭtio	-ēre	concussi	concussum	*shake together*
		-vi	**-tum**	
sĕro	ēre	sēvi	sătum	*sow*
sperno	-ĕre	sprēvi	sprētum	*despise*
cognosco	ēre	cognōvi	cognĭtum	*know*
cresco	-ēre	crēvi	crētum	*grow*
nosco	-ēre	nōvi	nōtum	*know*
		-īvī	**-ītum**	
quaero	-ēre	quaesivi	quaesitum	*seek*

Present	Infin.	Perfect	Supine	
		-ui	-tum	
cŏlo	-ĕre	colui	cultum	*till, worship*
răpio	-ĕre	rapui	raptum	*seize*
pōno	-ĕre	posui	positum	*place*
		-ī	-tum	

(a) Reduplicated -tum

căno	-ĕre	cĕcĭni	cantum	*sing*
tango	-ĕre	tĕtĭgĭ	tactum	*touch*
tendo	-ĕre	tĕtendi	tentum (tensum)	*stretch*
disco	-ĕre	dĭdĭci	—	*learn*
părio	-ĕre	pĕpĕri	partum	*bring forth*
			-sum	
cădo	-ĕre	cĕcĭdi	cāsum	*fall*
caedo	-ĕre	cĕcīdi	caesum	*beat, kill*
curro	-ĕre	cucurri	cursum	*run*
fallo	-ĕre	fĕfelli	falsum	*deceive*
părco	-ĕre	pĕperci	parsum	*spare*
pello	-ĕre	pĕpŭli	pulsum	*drive*
pendo	-ĕre	pĕpendi	pensum	*hang*

Some Compounds of dŏ.

addo	-ĕre	addidi	additum	*add*
condo	-ĕre	condidi	conditum	*found, hide*
crēdo	-ĕre	crēdidi	crēditum	*believe*
ēdo	-ĕre	ēdidi	ēditum	*give forth*
perdo	-ĕre	perdidi	perditum	*lose*
reddo	-ĕre	reddidi	redditum	*restore*
vendo	-ĕre	vendidi	venditum	*sell*

(b) Lengthened Stem -tum

emo	-ĕre	ēmi	emptum	*buy*
lĕgo	-ĕre	lēgi	lectum	*choose, read*
rumpo	-ĕre	rūpi	ruptum	*break*
vinco	-ĕre	vīci	victum	*conquer*
fŭgio	-ĕre	fūgi	fugitum	*fly*
ăgo	-ĕre	ēgi	actum	*do*
frango	-ĕre	frēgi	fractum	*break* (tr.)
făcio	-ĕre	fēci	factum	*make*
jăcio	-ĕre	jēci	jactum	*throw*
fundo	-ĕre	fūdi	fusum	*pour*
ĕdo	-ĕre	ēdi	esum	*eat*
		-ī	-tum, -sum	
bĭbo	-ĕre	bĭbi	bibitum	*drink*
verto	-ĕre	verti	versum	*turn* (tr.)

U- Stems. -i -tum

induo	-ĕre	indui	indutum	*put on*
statuo	-ĕre	statui	statutum	*set up*
solvo	-ĕre	solvi	solutum	*loosen, pay*
volvo	-ĕre	volvi	volutum	*roll* (tr.)

112　　　　　　　　　　**IV. I- Stems.**

Present	*Infin.*	*Perfect*	*Supine*
		Usual Form.	
-ĭō (-i-io)	**-īre**	**-īvī**	**-ītum**
audio	audīre	audīvi	audītum
		Exceptions.	
		-vi	**-tum**
scio	-īre	scivi	scitum	*know*
		-ui	**-tum**
apĕrio	-īre	aperui	apertum	*open*
		-si	**-tum**
haurio	-īre	hausi	haustum	*drain*
vincio	-īre	vinxi	vinctum	*bind*
		-si	**-sum**
sentio	-īre	sensi	sensum	*feel*
		-i	**-tum**
vĕnio	-īre	vēni	ventum	*come*
repĕrio	-īre	repperi	repertum	*discover*

DEPONENT VERBS.

113　　　　　　　**E- Stems (Perfect -ĭtus sum).**

Present	*Infin.*	*Perfect*	
vĕreor	-ērī	veritus sum	*fear*
reor	-ērī	rătus sum	*think*

114　　　　　　　　　**Semi-deponent Verbs.**

audeo	-ēre	ausus sum	—	*dare*
sŏleo	-ēre	sŏlitus sum	—	*be wont*

115　　**Consonant and U- Stems (Perfect -tŭs or -sŭs sum)**

fungor	-ī	functus sum	*perform*
ĭrascor	-ī	iratus sum	*be angry*
morior	-ĭ	mortuus sum	*die*
nascor	-ī	natus sum	*be born*
pătior	-ī	passus sum	*suffer*
proficiscor	-ī	profectus sum	*set out*
quĕror	-ī	questus sum	*complain*
ūtor	-ī	usus sum	*use*
lŏquor	-ī	locutus sum	*speak*
sĕquor	-ī	secutus sum	*follow*

116　　　　**I- Stems (Perfect -ĭtus, -tŭs or -sŭs sum).**

expĕrior	-īrī	expertus sum	*try*
ŏrior	-īri	ortus sum	*arise*
ordior	-īrī	orsus sum	*begin*
potior	-īrī	potītus sum	*acquire*

SYNTAX.

THE SIMPLE SENTENCE.

Introductory Outline.

117 SYNTAX teaches how **Sentences** are made.

Sentences are **Simple** or **Compound**.

118 A Simple Sentence has two parts:

1. The **Subject**: the person or thing spoken about;
2. The **Predicate**: that which is said about the Subject.

119 1. The **Subject** must be a **Substantive**, or some word or words taking the place of a Substantive:

A **Substantive**: lex, *the law.*

A **Substantive Pronoun**: ego, *I.*

An **Adjective, Participle,** or **Adjectival Pronoun**: Romanus, *a Roman*; iratus, *an angry man*; ille, *that (man).*

A **Verb Noun Infinitive**: navigare, *to sail* or *sailing.*

120 2. The **Predicate** must either be a **Verb** or contain a Verb, because it makes a statement or assertion about the Subject; and it is usually a Verb Finite, which alone has the power of making direct statements.

EXAMPLES OF THE SIMPLE SENTENCE.

Subject.	Predicate.	Subject.	Predicate.
Lex	jubet.	Nos	paremus.
Law	*commands.*	*We*	*obey.*

A single Verb may be a sentence. Veni, vidi, vici, *I came, I saw, I conquered,* comprises three sentences.

121   Some Verbs cannot by themselves form complete Predicates. The Verb sum is a complete Predicate only when it implies mere existence :

Seges   est   ubi   Troja   fuit.
Corn   is   where   Troy   was.

It more often links the Subject with the **Complement**, which completes what is said about it.

122   Verbs which link a Subject and Complement are called **Copulative Verbs.** Others besides sum are :

appareo, *appear* ;   audio, *am called* ; maneo, *remain* ;
evado, existo, *turn out* ;   videor, *seem.*

The Passives of Verbs of *making, saying, thinking* (**Factitive Verbs [134]**) are also used as Copulative Verbs :

fio (facio), *become* or *am made* ;   feror, *am reported* ;
appellor, *am called* ;   legor, *am chosen* ;
creor, *am created* ;   putor, *am thought* ;
declaror, *am declared* ;   vocor, *am called.*

Copulative Verbs have the same case after them as before them.

123   The Complement may be—

An **Adjective**, or a Participle or Pronoun used as an Adjective.

A Substantive.

Subject.	Predicate.	
	Copulative Verb.	Complement.
1. Leo	est	validus.
The lion	*is*	*strong.*
2. Illi	appellantur	philosophi.
They	*are called*	*philosophers.*

124   Many Verbs usually require another Verb in the Infinitive to carry on their construction : as soleo, *am wont* ; possum, *am able* ; queo, *can* ; debeo, *ought* ; volo, *wish* ; conor, *try.*

Solet legere.   Possum ire.
He is wont to read.   I am able to go.

These Verbs are called **Indeterminate**, and the Infinitive following them is called **Prolative**, because it carries on (profert) their construction.

AGREEMENT.

Rules of the Four Concords.

125   I. A Verb agrees with its Subject in Number and Person:

Tempus fugit.   Libri leguntur.
Time flies.   *Books are read.*

126   II. An Adjective or Participle agrees in Gender, Number and Case with the Substantive it qualifies:

Vir bonus bonam uxorem habet.
The good man has a good wife.

Verae amicitiae sempiternae sunt.   Cic.
True friendships are everlasting.

127   III. When a Substantive or Pronoun is followed by another Substantive, so that the second explains or describes the first, and has the same relation to the rest of the sentence, the second Noun agrees in Case with the first, and is said to be in Apposition:

Procas rex Albanorum, duos filios, Numitorem et
   Amulium, habuit.   Liv.
Procas, king of the Albans, had two sons, Numitor and Amulius.

128   IV. The Relative **qui, quae, quod,** agrees with its Antecedent in Gender, Number and Person; in Case it takes its construction from its own clause:

Amo te, mater, quae me amas.
I love you, mother, who love me.

Quis hic est homo quem ante aedes video?   Plaut.
Who is this man whom I see before the house?

Arbores multas serit agricola, quarum fructus non adspiciet.
   Cic.
The farmer plants many trees, of which he will not see the fruit.

129   COMPOSITE SUBJECT.

1. When two or more Nouns are united as the Subject, the Verb and Adjectives are usually in the Plural:

> Veneno absumpti sunt Hannibal et Philopoemen. **Liv.**
> *Hannibal and Philopoemen were cut off by poison.*

2. If the Persons of a Composite Subject are different, the Verb agrees with the first person rather than the second; with the second rather than the third:

> Si tu et Tullia valetis, ego et Cicero valemus. **Cic.**
> *If you and Tullia are well, I and Cicero are well.*

3. When the Genders are different, Adjectives agree with the Masculine rather than with the Feminine:

> ·Rex regiaque classis una profecti. **Liv.**
> *The king and the royal fleet set out together.*

4. If the things expressed are without life, the Adjectives are generally Neuter:

> Regna, honores, divitiae, caduca et incerta sunt. **Cic.**
> *Kingdoms, honours, riches, are frail and fickle things.*

THE CASES.

THE NOMINATIVE AND VOCATIVE CASES.

130   The Subject of a Finite Verb is in the Nominative Case:

> Anni fugiunt.   Labitur aetas. Ov.
> *Years flee.*   *Time glides away.*

131   A Substantive joined to the Subject by a Copulative Verb is in the Nominative Case:

> Cicero declaratus est consul. **Cic.**
> *Cicero was declared consul.*

132   The Vocative is used with or without an Interjection (233):

> O sol pulcher! *O beauteous sun!*   Pompei! *O Pompeius!*

The Accusative Case.

Accusative of Nearer Object.

133 The nearer Object of a Transitive Verb is in the Accusative Case:

> Agricola colit agros; uxor domum tuetur.
> *The farmer tills the fields; his wife takes care of the house.*

134 Factitive Verbs (verbs of *making, saying, thinking*) have a second Accusative, in agreement with the Object:

> Ciceronem consulem populus declaravit. SALL.
> *The people declared Cicero consul.*

> *Note.*—The Accusative is used with the Infinitive to form a Clause (240).
> Solem fulgere videmus. *We see that the sun shines.*

135 Some Verbs of *teaching, asking, concealing,* doceo, *teach,* flagito, *demand,* rogo, *ask,* oro, *pray,* celo, *conceal,* take two Accusatives, one of the Person, the other of the Thing:

> Racilius primum me sententiam rogavit. Cic.
> *Racilius asked me first my opinion.*

> *Note 1.*—In the Passive the Accusative of the Thing is sometimes kept:
> Primus a Racilio sententiam rogatus sum.
> *I was asked my opinion first by Racilius.*

> *Note 2.*—Quaero, peto, take Ablative of the Person, with *a* or *b*: hoc a te peto, *this I ask of you.*

136 Place to which **Motion** is directed is in the Accusative: eo Romam, *I go to Rome* (180, 181 c).

Cognate Accusative.

137 Many Intransitive Verbs take an Accusative containing the same idea as the Verb:

> Fortuna ludum insolentem ludit. HOR.
> *Fortune plays an insolent game.*

Adverbial Accusative.

138 The Accusative of Respect is joined to Verbs and Adjectives, especially in poetry:

> Tremit artus. VERG.   Nudae lacertos. TAC.
> *He trembles in his limbs.*   *Bare as to the arms.*

(For Accusative of Extent see 185. 186. 187.)

The Dative Case.

139   The Dative is the Case of the Person or Thing *to* or *for* whom or which something is done.

Dative of the Remoter Object.

The Dative of the Remoter Object is used:

140   (1) With Transitive Verbs of *giving, telling, showing, promising*; which take also an Accusative of the Nearer Object:

> Tibi librum sollicito damus aut fesso. Hor.
> *We give you a book when you are anxious or weary.*

> Saepe tibi meum somnium narravi. Cic.
> *I have often told you my dream.*

141   (2) With Intransitive Verbs of *pleasing, helping, sparing, pardoning, appearing, believing, obeying*, and their opposites:

> Imperio parent. Caes.   Parce pio generi. Verg.
> *They obey the command.*   *Spare a pious race.*

Note.—These Verbs contain the ideas of *being pleasing to, helpful to, obedient to*, &c.

142   *Note.*—Delecto, juvo, *delight*, laedo, *hurt*, guberno, *govern*, rego, *rule*, jubeo, *command*, take an accusative :

> Multos castra juvant. Hor.   Animum rege. Hor.
> *The camp delights many.*   *Rule the temper.*

Tempero, moderor, *govern, restrain*, take sometimes the accusative, sometimes the dative :

> Hic moderatur equos qui non moderabitur irae. Hor.
> *This man controls horses who will not restrain his anger.*

143   (3) With Adjectives implying *nearness, fitness, likeness, help, kindness, trust, obedience*, or any opposite idea :

> Quis amicior quam frater fratri? Sall.
> *Who (is) more friendly than a brother to a brother?*

> Homini fidelissimi sunt equus et canis. Plin.
> *The horse and the dog are most faithful to man.*

144 Many Verbs, Transitive and Intransitive, are used with a Dative of the Remoter Object when compounded with the following Prepositions :

ad, ante, ab,	sub, super, ob,
in, inter, de,	con, post, and prae.

And with the Adverbs bene, male, satis.

(*a*) Transitive :

Gigantes bellum dis intulerunt. CIC.
The giants waged war against the gods.

(*b*) Intransitive :

His negotiis non interfuit solum sed praefuit. CIC.
He not only took part in these affairs, but directed them.
Ceteris satisfacio semper, mihi nunquam. CIC.
I always satisfy others, myself never.

Dative of Advantage.

145 The person or thing for whose advantage or disadvantage something is done is in the Dative Case :

Tibi aras, tibi seris, tibi eidem metis. PLAUT.
For yourself you plough, for yourself you sow, for the same self you reap.

Non solum nobis divites esse volumus. CIC.
We do not wish to be rich for ourselves alone.

146 **Dative of the Possessor**, with esse :

Est mihi plenus Albani cadus. HOR.
I have a cask full of Alban wine. (lit. *there is to me.*)

147 A Dative is used to express **Result** or the **Purpose of** action.

Exitio est avidum mare nautis. HOR.
The greedy sea is a destruction to sailors.
Equitatum auxilio Caesari miserunt. CAES.
They sent the cavalry as a help to Caesar.

THE ABLATIVE CASE.

148 The Ablative is the Case which defines circumstances; it is rendered by many prepositions, *from, with, by, in.*

Ablative of Separation.

149 The **Ablative of Separation** is used with Verbs meaning *to remove, release, deprive*; with Adjectives, as liber, *free,* and the Adverb procul, *far from:*

> Populus Atheniensis Phocionem patriā pepulit. NEP.
> *The Athenian people drove Phocion from his country.*

150 The **Ablative of Comparison** (expressing Difference) is used with Comparative Adjectives and Adverbs:

> Nihil est amabilius virtute. CIC.
> *Nothing is more amiable than virtue.*

Note.—This construction is equivalent to quam, *than*, with the Nominative or Accusative. 'Virtute' equals 'quam virtus.'

(For **Place Whence** see 179, 181*b*).

Ablative of Association.

151 The **Ablative of Association** is used with Verbs and Adjectives denoting *plenty, fulness, possession*: abundo, *abound*, dono, *present*, praeditus, *endowed with* (**169**):

> Villa abundat porco, gallina, lacte, caseo, melle. CIC.
> *The farm abounds in pork, poultry, milk, cheese, honey.*
> Juvenem praestanti munere donat. VERG.
> *He presents the youth with a noble gift.*

152 The **Ablative of Quality** is used with an Adjective in agreement (**171**):

> Senex promissā barbā, horrenti capillo. PLIN. MIN.
> *An old man with long beard and rough hair.*

153 **Ablative of Respect:**

> Pauci numero.   Natione Medus.
> *Few in number.*   *By birth a Mede.*

154   The **Ablative of the Manner** in which something happens
or is done has an Adjective in agreement with it; or it
follows the Preposition **cum,** *with* :

> Jam veniet tacito curva senecta pede.. Ov.
> *Presently bent old age will come with silent foot.*
> Magnā cum curā atque diligentiā scripsit. Cic.
> *He wrote with great care and attention.*

155   The **Ablative Absolute** is a phrase consisting of a Noun
in the Ablative Case and a Participle, or another Noun, in
agreement with it : it is called Absolute because in construc=
tion it is independent of the rest of the Sentence :

> Regibus exactis consules creati sunt. Liv.
> *Kings having been abolished, consuls were elected.*
> Nil desperandum Teucro duce. Hor.
> *There must be no despair, Teucer being leader.*

Instrumental Ablative.

156   The **Agent**, by whom something is done, is in the Ablative,
with the Preposition **a, ab,** after a Passive Verb **(194)**.

157   The **Instrument** by means of which something is done is
in the Ablative Case without a Preposition :

> Hi jaculis, illi certant defendere saxis. Verg.
> *These strive to defend with javelins, those with stones.*

158   The **Ablative of the Cause** is used with Adjectives, Passive Participles, and Verbs :

> Oderunt peccare mali formidine poenae. Hor.
> *The bad hate to sin through fear of punishment.*

159   The Deponent Verbs fungor, *perform,* fruor, *enjoy,*
vescor, *feed on,* utor, *use,* potior, *possess oneself of* **(169)**,
take an Ablative :

> Numidae ferina carne vescebantur. Sall.
> *The Numidians used to feed on the flesh of wild animals.*

160   The Adjectives dignus, *worthy,* indignus, *unworthy,* and
the Transitive Verb dignor, *deem worthy,* also contentus,
contented, and fretus, *relying on,* take an Ablative :

> Dignum laude virum Musa vetat mori. Hor.
> *A man worthy of praise the Muse forbids to die.*

161   An **Ablative of the Measure of difference** is joined with Comparatives and Superlatives, and, rarely, with Verbs:

> Hibernia dimidio minor est quam Britannia.   CAES.
> *Ireland is smaller by half than Britain.*

162   The **Ablative of Price** is used with Verbs and Adjectives of *buying* and *selling*:

> Vendidit hic auro patriam.   VERG.
> *This man sold his country for gold.*

The Locative Ablative.

163   The **Locative** is the Case of the **Place at which** something is or happens.   Its distinct forms remain in the Singular in names of towns and small islands: Romae, *at Rome*; Corcyrae, *at Corcyra*; and in a few other words, as domi, *at home*.   For the most part its uses have passed to the Ablative, and it is often difficult to distinguish between the two Cases, especially in the Plural, where their forms are identical.   (For **Place where**, see **178, 181** *a.*)

THE GENITIVE CASE.

164   The Genitive is used to define or complete the meaning of another Noun on which it depends.   It also follows certain Verbs.

165   The **Genitive of Definition** follows the Noun on which it depends:

> Vox voluptatis.   Nomen regis.
> *The word pleasure.*   *The name of king.*

> *Note.*—But the name of a city is always placed in Apposition: urbs Roma, *the city of Rome.*

166   The **Attributive Genitive** defines the Noun on which it depends like an Adjective:

> Lux solis.   Anni labor.
> *The light of the sun.*   *A year's toil.*

167   The **Genitive of the Author**:

> Ea statua dicebatur esse Myronis.   CIC.
> *That statue was said to be Myro's.*

168   Verbs and Adjectives of *accusing, condemning, convicting,*
or *acquitting* take a Genitive of the fault or crime :

> Alter latrocinii reus, alter caedis convictus est. CIC.
> *The one was accused of robbery, the other was convicted of murder.*

169   Verbs and Adjectives implying *want* and *fulness,* especially egeo, indigeo, *want,* impleo, *fill,* potior, *get possession
of,* plenus, *full,* often take a Genitive ; (151, 159.)

> Indigeo tui consilii. CIC.   Acerra turis plena. HOR.
> *I need your advice.*   *A pan full of incense.*

> Signorum potiti sunt. SALL.
> *They got possession of the standards.*

170   **Possessive Genitive:**

> Regis copiae. CIC.   Contempsi Catilinae gladios. CIC.
> *The king's forces.*   *I have braved the swords of Catiline.*

171   The **Genitive of Quality** has an Adjective in agreement :

> Ingenui vultus puer ingenuique pudoris. JUV.
> *A boy of noble countenance and noble modesty.*

172   **Genitives of Value,** magni, parvi, plurimi, minimi, nihili,
are used with verbs of *valuing* and *weighing* :

> Voluptatem sapiens minimi facit.
> *The wise man accounts pleasure of very little value.*

Partitive Genitive.

173   The Genitive of a Noun which is distributed into parts
is called a Partitive Genitive.

> Sulla centum viginti suorum amisit. EUT.
> *Sulla lost a hundred and twenty of his men*

> Multae harum arborum mea manu sunt satae. CIC.
> *Many of these trees were planted by my hand.*

The Objective Genitive.

174   *Note.*—The terms Subjective and Objective Genitive are used to express different relations of the Genitive to the Noun on which it depends. Thus amor patris, *the love of a father,* may mean either 'the love felt *by* a father' (where patris is a Subjective Genitive), or 'the love felt *for* a father' (where patris is an Objective Genitive).

175   An Objective Genitive is used with Verbal Substantives, Adjectives, and Participles which have the meaning of *love, desire, hope, fear, care, knowledge, skill, power :*

With Substantives :

> Erat insitus menti cognitionis amor. Cic.
> *Love of knowledge had been implanted in the mind*

With Adjectives and Participles :

> Avida est periculi virtus. Sen.
> *Valour is greedy of danger.*

> Quis famulus amantior domini quam canis? Col.
> *What servant is fonder of his master than the dog is ?*

176   Most Verbs of *remembering, forgetting, reminding,* memini, reminiscor, obliviscor, usually take the Genitive, sometimes the Accusative. Recordor almost always takes the Accusative, rarely the Genitive :

> Animus meminit praeteritorum. Cic.
> *The mind remembers past things.*
> Nam modo vos animo dulces reminiscor, amici. Ov.
> *For now I remember you, O friends, dear to my soul.*

177   The Adjectives corresponding to these Verbs, memor, immemor, always take a Genitive :

> Omnes immemorem beneficii oderunt. Cic.
> *All hate one who is forgetful of a kindness.*

Verbs of *pitying,* misereor, miseresco, take a Genitive :

> Nil nostri miserere. Verg.
> *You pity me not at all.*
> Arcadii, quaeso, miserescite regis. Verg.
> *Take pity, I entreat, on the Arcadian king.*

Note —Miseror, commiseror take an Accusative.

PLACE, TIME, AND SPACE.

Place.

178 Place where anything is or happens is generally in the Ablative Case with the Preposition *in*; sometimes without a Preposition, (especially in Poetry), an Adjective of place being attached to the Substantive:

Castra sunt in Italiā contra rempublicam collocata. CIC.
A camp has been formed in Italy against the republic.

Medio sedet insula ponto. Ov.
The island lies in mid ocean.

179 Place whence there is motion is in the Ablative with **ab,** **ex,** or **de**:

Ex Asiā transis in Europam. CURT.
Out of Asia you cross into Europe.

180 Place whither is in the Accusative with a Preposition:

Caesar in Italiam magnis itineribus contendit. CAES.
Caesar hastened into Italy with long marches.

181 In names of **towns** and **small islands**, also in **domus**, and **rus**, Place where, whence, or whither is expressed by the Case without a Preposition.

(*a*) **Place where,** by the Locative:

Quid Romae faciam? Juv. | Is habitat Mileti. TER.
What am I to do at Rome? | *He lives at Miletus.*

Philippus Neapoli est, Lentulus Puteolis. CIC.
Philip is at Naples, Lentulus at Puteoli.

Est mihi namque domi pater, est injusta noverca. VERG.
I have at home a father and an unjust stepmother.

(*b*) **Place whence,** by the Ablative:

Demaratus fugit Tarquinios Corintho. CIC.
Demaratus fled from Corinth to Tarquinii.

(c) Place whither, by the Accusative:

Regulus Carthaginem rediit.   Cɪᴄ.
Regulus returned to Carthage.

Vos ite domum; ego rus ibo.
Go ye home: I will go into the country.

182   **The road by which one goes is in the Ablative:**

Ibam forte Viā Sacrā.   Hoʀ.
I was going by chance along the Sacred Way.

Time.

183 Time at which, in answer to the question When? is expressed by the Ablative: hieme, *in winter*; solis occasu, *at sunset*:

-Ego Capuam veni eo ipso die.   Cɪᴄ.
I came to Capua on that very day.

184 Time within which, generally by the Ablative:

Quicquid est biduo sciemus.   Cɪᴄ.
Whatever it is, we shall know in two days.

185 Time during which, generally by the Accusative:

Pericles quadraginta annos praefuit Athenis.   Cɪᴄ.
Pericles was leader of Athens forty years.

Space.

186 Space over which motion takes place is in the Accusative:

Milia tum pransi tria repimus.   Hoʀ.
Then having had luncheon we crawl three miles.

187 Space of measurement, answering the questions How high? How deep? How broad? How long? is generally in the Accusative:

Erant muri Babylonis ducenos pedes alti.   Pʟɪɴ.
The walls of Babylon were two hundred feet high.

PREPOSITIONS.

188 With Accusative:

antĕ, ăpŭd, ăd, adversŭs,
circum, circā, citrā, cĭs,
contrā, intĕr, ergā, extrā,
infrā, intrā, juxtā, ŏb,
pĕnĕs, pōnĕ, post, and praetĕr,
prŏpĕ, proptĕr, pĕr, sĕcundum,
suprā, versŭs, ultrā, trans :
Add sŭpĕr, subtĕr, sŭb and in,
When ' *motion* ' 'tis, not ' *state,* '
they mean.

before, near, to, towards,
around, about, on this side of,
against, between, towards, outside of,
beneath, within, beside, on account of,
in the power of, behind, after, along,
near, on account of, through, next to,
above, towards, beyond, across :
Add *over, underneath, under, into,*
When they mean ' *motion,* ' not
' *state.* '

189 With Ablative:

ā, ăb, absquĕ, cōram, dē,

pălam, clam, cum, ex, and ē,
sĭnĕ, tĕnŭs, prō, and prae :
Add sŭpĕr, subtĕr, sŭb and in,
When ' *state,* ' not ' *motion,* ' 'tis they
mean.

by, from, without, in the presence of
from,
in sight of, unknown to, with, out of,
without, as far as, for, before :
Add *over, underneath, under, in,*
When they mean ' *state,* ' not ' *mo-*
tion. '

Clam sometimes takes the Accusative.

IMPERSONAL VERBS.

Case Construction.

190 The following verbs of *feeling* take an Accusative of the person with a Genitive of the cause : miseret, piget, paenitet, pudet, taedet :

> Miseret te aliorum, tui te nec miseret nec pudet. PLAUT.
> *You pity others, for yourself you have neither pity nor shame.*

191 Libet, licet take a Dative :

> Ne libeat tibi quod non licet. CIC.
> *Let not that please you which is not lawful.*

192   Interest, *it is of importance, it concerns*, is used with the Genitive of the person or thing concerned, but with the feminine Ablatives meā, tuā, suā, nostrā, vestrā of the Possessive Pronouns :

> Interest omnium recte facere.   Cic.
> *It is for the good of all to do right.*

> Et tuā et meā interest te valere.   Cic.
> *It is of importance to you and to me that you should be well.*

193   Rēfert, *it concerns, it matters*, is also used with the feminine Ablatives of the Possessive Pronouns :

> Quid meā rēfert cui serviam?   Phaed.
> *What does it matter to me whom I serve ?*

PASSIVE CONSTRUCTION.

When a sentence is changed from the Active to the Passive form :

194   The Object of a Transitive Verb becomes the Subject ; the Subject becomes the Agent in the Ablative with the Preposition a or ab :

> Numa leges dedit.   *Numa gave laws.*
> A Numā leges datae sunt.   *Laws were given by Numa.*

195   Intransitive Verbs are used impersonally in the Passive :

> Nos currimus.   Cic.   *We run.*
> A nobis curritur.   lit. *There is running (done) by us.*

or the Agent may be omitted :

> Sic imus ad astra. ⎫   *Thus we go to the stars.*
> Sic itur ad astra. ⎭

PRONOUNS.

196 The Reflexive Pronoun **se, sese, sui, sibi, in a Simple** Sentence refers to a Subject in the Third Person :

Fur telo se defendit. Cic.	Ira sui impotens est. Sen.
The thief defends himself with a weapon.	*Anger is not master of itself.*

197 The Possessive **suus**, formed from the Reflexive, is used to express *his own, their own,* when emphasis is required, and usually refers to the Subject of the Verb :

Nemo rem suam emit.
No one buys what is his own.

sometimes to other cases if the context shows that it cannot be referred to the Subject :

Apibus fructum restituo suum. Phaedr.
I restore to the bees their own produce.

198 Ejus is the Possessive used of the Third Person where no emphasis is required. It never refers to the Subject of the Sentence.

Chilius te rogat, et ego ejus rogatu. Cic.
Chilius asks you, and I (ask you) at his request.

199 Hic, ille are often used in contrast : hic usually meaning *the latter,* ille *the former* :

Quocumque adspicio, nihil est nisi pontus et aer,
  nubibus hic tumidus, fluctibus ille minax. Ov.
*Whithersoever I look, there is naught but sea and sky,
  the latter heaped with clouds, the former threatening with billows.*

200 Ipse, *self,* is used of all the three Persons, with or without a Personal Pronoun : ipse ibo, *I will go myself.*

Of the Indefinite Pronouns :—

201 Aliquis means *some one* : dicat aliquis, *suppose some one to say.*

202 Quidam means *a certain person* (known but not named) · vir quidam, *a certain man.*

203 Quisquam (Substantive), } *any at all,*
Ullus (Adjective) : }

> are often·used after a negative word, or in a question expecting a negative answer:
>
> Nec amet quemquam nec ametur ab ullo. **Juv.**
> *Let him not love anyone nor be loved by any.*
>
> Non ullus aratro dignus honos. **Verg.**
> *Not any due honour to the plough.*

204 Quivis, quilibet, *any you like* :

> Non cuivis homini contingit adire Corinthum. **Hor.**
> *It does not happen to every man to go to Corinth.*

205 Quisque, *each* (severally), is often used with se, suus :

> Sibi quisque habeant quod suum est. **Plaut.**
> *Let them have each for himself what is his own.*

206 Uterque, *each* (of two), *both,* can be used with the Genitive of Pronouns; but with Substantives it agrees in case :

> Uterque parens. **Ov.** | Utroque vestrum delector. **Cic.**
> *Both father and mother.* | *I am delighted with both of you.*

207 Uter, *which* (of two), is Interrogative : uter melior? *which is the better?*

> Uter utri insidias fecit? **Cic.**
> *Which laid an ambush for which?*

208 Alter, *the one, the other* (of two), *the second,* is the Demonstrative of uter : alter ego, alter idem, *a second self* :

> Quicquid negat alter, et alter. **Hor.**
> *Whatever the one denies, so does the other.*

209 Alius, *another* (of any number), *different* :

> Fortuna nunc mihi, nunc alii benigna. **Hor.**
> *Fortune, kind now to me, now to another.*

THE VERB INFINITE.

210   The parts of the Verb Infinite have some of the uses of Verbs, some of the uses of Nouns.

211   The **Infinitive** as a Verb has Tenses, Present, Past, and Future, it governs Cases and is qualified by Adverbs ; as a Noun it is neuter, and indeclinable, used only as Nominative or Accusative.

212   As Nominative :

> Juvat ire et Dorica castra visere.   VERG.
> *To go and view the Doric camp is pleasant.*

> Non vivere bonum est sed bene vivere.   SEN.
> *It is not living which is a good, but living well.*

213   As Accusative :

> Errare, nescire, decipi, et malum et turpe ducimus.   CIC.
> *To err, to be ignorant, to be deceived, we deem both unfortunate and disgraceful.*

214   The Prolative Infinitive is often used to carry on the construction of Indeterminate and some other Verbs :

> Solent diu cogitare qui magna volunt gerere.   CIC.
> *They are wont to reflect long who wish to do great things.*

GERUND AND GERUNDIVE.

215   The Genitive, Dative, and Ablative of the **Gerund**, and the Accusative with a Preposition, are used as Cases of the Infinitive.

216   The **Accusative** of the Gerund follows some Prepositions, usually ad, sometimes ob, inter :

> Ad bene vivendum breve tempus satis est longum.   CIC.
> *For living well a short time is long enough.*

> Mores puerorum se inter ludendum detegunt.   QUINT.
> *The characters of boys show themselves in their play.*

217   The **Genitive** of the Gerund is used after some Substantives and Adjectives:

Ars scribendi discitur. | Cupidus te audiendi sum. Cic.
The art of writing is learnt. | *I am desirous of hearing you.*

218   The **Dative** of the Gerund follows a few Verbs, Adjectives, and Substantives, implying *help, use, fitness*:

Par est disserendo. Cic. | Dat operam legendo.
He is equal to arguing. | *He gives attention to reading.*

219   The **Ablative** of the Gerund is of Cause or Means, or it follows one of the Prepositions in ab, de, ex:

Fugiendo vincimus. | De pugnando deliberant.
We conquer by flying. | *They deliberate about fighting.*

220   If the Verb is Transitive, the Gerundive is used, agreeing with the Object as an Adjective. It takes the Gender and Number of the Object, but the Object is drawn into the Case of the Gerundive.

The following examples show how the Gerundive is used:

Gerundive.

ad petendam pacem   *in order to seek peace.*
petendae pacis   *of seeking peace.*
petenda pace   *by seeking peace.*
ad mutandas leges   *in order to change laws.*
mutandarum legum   *of changing laws.*
mutandis legibus   *for or by changing laws.*

221   The Gerund and Gerundive are often used to express that something must or ought to be done, the Dative of the Agent being expressed or understood.

222   If the Verb is **Intransitive** the Gerund is used impersonally:

Eundum est. | Mihi eundum est.
One must go. | *I must go.*

223   If the Verb is **Transitive** the Gerundive is used in agreement:

Caesari omnia uno tempore erant agenda. Caes.
All things had to be done by Caesar at one time.

SUPINES.

224 The Supines are also used as Cases of the Infinitive:

225 The Supine in -ŭm is an Accusative after Verbs of motion, expressing the purpose:

> Lusum it Maecenas, dormitum ego. HOR.
> *Maecenas goes to play, I to sleep.*

with the Infinitive iri, used impersonally, it forms the Future Passive Infinitive:

> Aiunt urbem captum iri.
> *They say that the city will be taken.*
> *Note.*—Literally, *they say there is a going to take the city.*

226 The Supine in -u Ablative or Dative is used with some Adjectives, such as facilis, dulcis, turpis, and the Substantives fas, nefas: turpe factu, *disgraceful to do.*

> Hoc fas est dictu. | Libertas, dulce auditu nomen. LIV.
> *It is lawful to say this.* | *Freedom, a name sweet to hear.*

ADVERBS.

227 Adverbs show how, when, and where the action of the Verb takes place; they also qualify Adjectives or other Adverbs: recte facere, *to do rightly*; huc nunc venire, *to come hither now*; facile primus, *easily first*; valde celeriter, *very swiftly.*

228 Negative Adverbs are non, haud, ne:

Non, *not,* is simply negative:

> Nives in alto mari non cadunt. PLIN.
> *No snow falls on the high seas.*

Haud, *not,* is used with Adjectives and with other Adverbs:

> Res haud dubia. | Haud aliter.
> *No doubtful matter.* | *Not otherwise.*

Ne is sometimes used with the second person of the Perfect Subjunctive for prohibitions: ne transieris Hiberum (LIV.), *do not cross the Ebro*; with the second person of the Present Subjunctive ne often means *lest*: ne forte credas (HOR.), *lest by chance you believe,* or *that you may not by chance believe.*

CONJUNCTIONS.

229   Conjunctions connect words, sentences and clauses, and are (1) **Co-ordinative**; (2) **Subordinative**.

230   (1) **Co-ordinative Conjunctions** connect two or more Nouns in the same Case:

> Miratur portas, strepitumque et strata viarum.   VERG.
> *He marvels at the gates and the noise and the pavements.*
>
> Aut Caesar, aut nullus.
> *Either Caesar or nobody.*

231   (2) **Subordinative Conjunctions** join Dependent Clauses to the Principal Sentence.   (See Compound Sentence.)

232   ### Co-ordination.

When two or more sentences are joined together by Co-ordinative Conjunctions, so as to form parts of one sentence, they are said to be **Co-ordinate Sentences**, and each is independent in its construction:

> Et mihi sunt vires et mea tela nocent.   Ov.
> *I too am not powerless, and my weapons hurt.*
>
> Gyges a nullo videbatur, ipse autem omnia videbat.   CIC.
> *Gyges was seen by no one, while he himself saw all things.*

INTERJECTIONS.

233   Interjections are apart from the construction of the sentence. O, ah, eheu, heu, **pro**, are used with the Vocative, Nominative or Accusative; en, ecce, with the Nominative or Accusative; ei, vae, with the Dative only:

> O formose puer!   VERG.   O fortunatam Romam!   CIC.
> *O beautiful boy!*   *O fortunate Rome!*
>
> En ego vester Ascanius!   VERG.
> *Lo here am I your Ascanius!*
>
> Vae victis!   LIV.
> *Woe to the vanquished!*

QUESTION.

234   (*a*) **Single Questions** are asked by :

nonně, expecting the answer *yes.*
num   ,,   ,,   ,,   *no.*
-ně, expecting either answer.

Canis nonne similis lupo est? Cic.
Is not a dog like a wolf?

Num negare audes? Cic. | Potesne dicere? Cic.
Do you venture to deny? | *Can you say?*

235   (*b*) **Alternative Questions** are most often asked by :

utrum ⎫
-ně   ⎬ an, anne (*or*), annon (*or not*).
      ⎭

Utrum ea vestra an nostra culpa est? Cic.
Is that your fault or ours?

Romamne venio, an hic maneo, an Arpinum fugio? Cic.
Do I come to Rome, or stay here, or flee to Arpinum?

THE COMPOUND SENTENCE.

236 A **Compound Sentence** consists of a Principal Sentence with one or more Subordinate Clauses.

237 Subordinate Clauses depend in their construction on the Principal Sentence. They are:

I. **Substantival.** II. **Adverbial.** III. **Adjectival.**

I. SUBSTANTIVAL CLAUSES.

238 A **Substantival Clause** stands like a Substantive, as Subject or Object of a Verb, or in Apposition.

239 Substantival Clauses have three forms, corresponding to the three Direct forms of the Simple Sentence.

(1) Indirect Statement; (2) Indirect Command or Request; (3) Indirect Question.

240 ### (1) Indirect Statement.

The **Accusative with Infinitive** is the most usual form of Indirect Statement:

| Valeo. } Direct | Scis me valere. } Indirect |
| *I am well.* } Statement. | *You know that I am well.* } Statement |

Nuntiatum est Scipionem adesse. **CAES.**
It was announced that Scipio was at hand.

Democritus dicit innumerabiles esse mundos. **CIC.**
Democritus says that there are countless worlds.

Illud temere dictum, sapientes omnes esse bonos. **CIC.**
It was rashly said that all wise men are good.

A Clause formed by **Ut** with the Subjunctive is sometimes used in Indirect Statement.

Expedit ut civitates sua jura habeant. **LIV.**
That states should have their own laws is expedient.

Sometimes a Clause formed by **Quod** with the Indicative is used instead of the Accusative with Infinitive, especially with Verbs of rejoicing and grieving:

Dolet mihi quod tu stomacharis. **CIC.**
It grieves me that you are angry.

241 ## (2) Indirect Command or Request.

A Clause depending on a Verb of *commanding, wishing, exhorting, entreating,* is in the Subjunctive; if positive, with **ut**; if negative, with **ne**:

Vale.	Direct	Cura ut valeas.	Indirect
Farewell.	Command.	*Take care that you keep well.*	Command.

Postulatur ab amico ut sit sincerus. Cic.
It is required of a friend that he be sincere.

Mihi ne abscedam imperat. Ter.
He commands me not to go away.

242 ## (3) Indirect Question.

Indirect Question is formed by an Interrogative Pronoun or Particle with a Verb in the Subjunctive:

Valesne?	Direct	Quaerorum valeas.	Indirect
Are you well ?	Question.	*I ask if you are well.*	Question.

Nescio quid facias.
I do not know what you are doing.

Fac me certiorem quando adfuturus sis. Cic.
Let me know when you are coming.

243 ## II. Adverbial Clauses.

Adverbial Clauses qualify like an Adverb, answering the questions *how, why, when,* and are joined to the Principal Sentence by Conjunctions. They are:

1. **Consecutive,** expressing *consequence,* joined by **ut,** *so that,* **ut non,** *so that . . . not,* with the Subjunctive:

Non sum ita hebes ut istud dicam. Cic.
I am not so stupid as to say that.

2. **Final,** expressing *purpose,* joined by **ut,** *in order that,* **ne,** *in order that . . . not,* with the Subjunctive:

Venio ut videam.	Abii ne viderem.
I come that I may see.	*I went away that I might not see*

3. **Causal,** giving a *reason,* joined by **quod, quia,** *because,* **quoniam, quando,** *since,* with the Indicative:

Ego primam tollo nominor quia Leo. Phaedr.
I take the first (share) because my name is Lion.

or by cum, *since,* with the Subjunctive :

> Quae cum ita sint, ab Jove veniam peto. Cic.
> *Since these things are so, I seek pardon of Jupiter.*

4. **Temporal,** shewing the *time,* joined by ubi, ut, cum, **quando,** *when,* **quotiens,** *as often as,* dum, donec, *while, until,* generally with the Indicative :

> Lituo Romulus regiones direxit tum cum urbem condidit. Cic.
> *Romulus marked out the districts with a staff at the time when he founded the city.*

In narrative **cum** is used with the Imperfect or Pluperfect Subjunctive :

> Cum ad oppidum venisset oppugnare instituit. Caes.
> *When he had come to the town, he began to attack it.*

5. **Conditional,** expressing a *condition,* joined by si, *if,* **nisi,** *unless.* If the condition is regarded as relating to an actual fact, the Indicative is used ; if to what is only possible or imaginary, the Subjunctive :

> Si vales, bene est. Cic.
> *If you are in good health, all is well.*

Si venias, gaudeam.	Si venisses, gavisus essem.
If you were to come, I should rejoice.	*If you had come, I should have rejoiced.*

6. **Concessive,** making a concession, joined by etsi, **etiamsi,** *even if, although,* **quamquam,** *although,* with the Indicative if something is granted as being true, with the Subjunctive if it is only granted for the sake of argument :

> Etiamsi tacent, satis dicunt. Cic.
> *Although they are silent, they say enough.*
>
> Etiamsi tacerent, satis dicerent.
> *Even if they were to be silent, they would say enough.*

7. **Comparative,** making an imaginary *comparison,* joined by quasi, tamquam, tamquam si, ut si, velut si, *as if,* with the Subjunctive :

> Tamquam si claudus sim, cum fusti est ambulandum. Plaut.
> *I must walk with a stick as if I were lame.*

244 ### III. ADJECTIVAL CLAUSES.

Adjectival Clauses qualify like an Adjective, and are joined to the Principal Sentence by the Relative **qui, quae, quod,** or by a Relative Particle with the Verb in the Indicative :

Est in Britannia flumen, qu od appellatur Tamesis. CAES.
There is in Britain a river which is called the Thames.

But the Relative or Relative Particle often forms a Clause, Consecutive, Final or Causal, with the Subjunctive, corresponding to the Adverbial Clauses of similar meaning:

Ea est Romana gens quae victa quiescere n e s c i a t. LIV.
The Roman race is such that it knows not how to rest quiet under defeat.

Legatos misit qui pacem peterent.
He sent ambassadors to seek peace.

245 ### Sequence of Tenses.

The general rule for the Sequence of Tenses is that a Primary Tense in the Principal Sentence is followed in the Clause by a Primary Tense (Present, Perfect, or Future), a Historic Tense by a Historic Tense (Imperfect, Pluperfect, or Future Perfect).

246 ### RULES FOR THE CHANGE OF DIRECT SPEECH INTO INDIRECT SPEECH (ORATIO OBLIQUA).

Oratio Obliqua is used in reports, whether short or long, of speeches, letters, &c.

247 In **Indirect Statement** the Principal Verbs are changed from the Indicative to the Infinitive in the same tense :

Direct.	*Indirect.*
Romulus urbem condidit.	Narrant Romulum urbem con- didisse.
Romulus founded the city.	*They say that Romulus founded the city.*

Note.—If the actual words of the speaker or writer are quoted, they are often introduced with **inquit,** *he says,* following the first word :

Romulus haec precatus, 'hinc,' inquit, 'Romani, Juppiter iterare pugnam jubet.' LIV.
When Romulus had thus prayed, 'Hence,' he says, 'Romans, Jupiter commands (you) to renew the battle.'

248   In **Indirect Commands** the **Subjunctive** (most commonly in the Imperfect, but sometimes in the Present Tense) takes the place of the Imperative in Direct Commands :

Ite, inquit, c r e a t e consules ex plebe.	(Hortatus est:) i r e n t, c r e a r e n t consules ex plebe.
Go, he says, and elect consuls from the plebs.	*He exhorted them to go and elect consuls from the plebs.*

249   In **Indirect Questions** the Verbs are in the Subjunctive (usually in the Imperfect or Pluperfect Tense, but sometimes in the Present or Perfect) :

Quid a g i s ? inquit.	Rogavit eum quid a g e r e t.
He says, ' What are you doing ?	*He asked him what he was doing.*
Clamavit ' Quid e g i s t i ? '	Quaesivit quid e g i s s e t.
He exclaimed, ' What have you done ? '	*He asked what he had done.*

250   The Pronoun which refers to the Subject of the Verb is the Reflexive **se** ; the Pronoun which refers to the Person spoken to is generally **ille** :

> Dicit Caesari Ariovistus nisi decedat s e s e i l l u m non pro amico, sed pro hoste habiturum.   Cᴀᴇꜱ.
>
> *Ariovistus says to Caesar that ' unless he departs he (Ariovistus) shall consider him (Caesar) not as a friend but as an enemy.'*

Sometimes **ipse** is used for the sake of clear distinction:

> Dicit Ariovistus transisse Rhenum s e s e non sua sponte sed roga-tum a Gallis ; sedes habere in Gallia ab i p s i s concessas.
>
> *Ariovistus says that he had crossed the Rhine, not of his own accord, but when asked by the Gauls ; that he had settlements in Gaul granted by themselves (the Gauls).*

251   In any Clause dependent on a Clause in Oratio Obliqua, the Verb must be in the Subjunctive :

Romulus urbem condidit q u a e R o m a appellatur.	Narratur Romulum urbem condi-disse q u a e R o m a appelletur.
Romulus founded the city which is called Rome.	*It is related that Romulus founded the city which is called Rome.*
Titum amo q u i a b o n u s e s t.	Dicit se Titum amare q u i a b o n u s sit.
I love Titus because he is good.	*He says that he loves Titus because he is good.*

252

Direct Statement.

Cum Germanis Haedui semel atque iterum armis contenderunt; magnam calamitatem pulsi accepperunt, omnem nobilitatem, omnem equitatum amiserunt. Sed pejus victoribus Sequanis quam Haeduis victis accidit; propterea quod Ariovistus, rex Germanorum, in eorum finibus consedit, tertiamque partem agri Sequani, qui est optimus totius Galliae, occupavit. Ariovistus barbarus, iracundus est, non possunt ejus imperia diutius sustineri.

The Haeduans have repeatedly fought with the Germans; they have been defeated and suffered great misfortune; they have lost all their nobles and all their cavalry. But worse has befallen the conquering Sequani than the conquered Haeduans, for Ariovistus, king of the Germans, has settled in their dominions and occupied a third part of their territory, which is the best in all Gaul. Ariovistus is barbarous and passionate; his commands can no longer be endured.

253

Direct Command.

Vestrae pristinae virtutis et tot secundissimorum proeliorum retinete memoriam, atque ipsum Caesarem, cujus ductu saepenumero hostes superavistis, praesentem adesse existimate.

Keep in mind your former valour and your many successful battles, and imagine that Caesar, under whose leadership you so often overcame your foes, is himself present.

Indirect Statement.

Locutus est pro Haeduis Divitiacus: Cum Germanis Haeduos semel atque iterum armis contendisse; magnam calamitatem pulsos accepisse, omnem nobilitatem, omnem equitatum amisisse. Sed pejus victoribus Sequanis quam Haeduis victis accidisse; propterea quod Ariovistus, rex Germanorum, in eorum finibus consedisset, tertiamque partem agri Sequani, qui esset optimus totius Galliae, occupavisset. Ariovistum esse barbarum, iracundum, non posse ejus imperia diutius sustineri.

Divitiacus said on behalf of the Haedui: 'That the Haedui had fought repeatedly with the Germans; that, having been defeated, they had suffered great misfortune (and) had lost all their nobles, all their cavalry. But that worse had befallen the conquering Sequani than the conquered Haeduans, for Ariovistus, king of the Germans, had settled in their dominions and had occupied a third part of their territory, which was the best in all Gaul. That Ariovistus was barbarous, passionate; and that his commands could no longer be endured.'

Indirect Command.

Labienus milites cohortatus ut suae pristinae virtutis et tot secundissimorum proeliorum retinerent memoriam, atque ipsum Caesarem, cujus ductu saepenumero hostes superassent, praesentem adesse existimarent, dat signum proelii.

Labienus, having exhorted the soldiers to keep in mind their former valour and their many successful battles, and to imagine that Caesar, under whose leadership they had so often overcome their foes, was himself present, gives the signal for battle.

RULES OF QUANTITY.

I. General Rules.

254

1. A syllable is short when it contains a short vowel followed by a simple consonant or by another vowel : as păter, dĕus.

2. A syllable is long when it contains a long vowel or diphthong : frātĕr, cāedēs, nēmo.

3. A vowel short by nature becomes long by position when it is followed by two consonants, or by x or z : cānto, sīmplēx, orȳza.

Exception.—A short vowel before a stop followed by a liquid becomes doubtful : lugŭbre, tenĕbrae, trĭplex.

4. A long vowel or diphthong becomes short before another vowel, or before h followed by a vowel : prŏavus, trăho, prăĕesse.

But in Greek words the vowel or diphthong keeps its length : āer, Aenēas, Enȳo, Melibōēus.

Exceptions.—In fīo, Gāius, Pompēi, dius, diēi, Rhēa (Silvia), the vowel remains long.

Note.—Prae in compounds is the only Latin word in which a diphthong occurs before a vowel.

5. A syllable is called doubtful when it is found in poetry to be sometimes long, sometimes short : Dĭana, fidĕi, rĕi, and genitives in -ius, as illĭus, except alĭus, alterĭus.

6. The quantity of a stem syllable is kept, as a rule, in compounds and derivatives : cădo occĭdo, rătus irrĭtus, flūmĕn flūmĭneus.

Exceptions to this rule are numerous :—lūceo, lŭcerna

255

II. Rule for Monosyllables.

Most monosyllables are long : dā, dēs, mē, vēr, sī, sīs, sōl, nōs, tū, mūs.

Exceptions :

Substantives : cŏr, fĕl, mĕl, ŏs (*bone*), vĭr.

Pronouns : ĭs, ĭd, quă (*any*), quĭs, quĭd, quŏd, quŏt, tŏt.

Verbs : dăt, dĕt, ĭt, scĭt, sĭt, stăt, stĕt, făc, fĕr, ĕs (from sum).

Particles : ăb, ăd, ăn, ăt, bĭs, cĭs, ĕt, ĭn, nĕc, ŏb, pĕr, pŏl, săt, sĕd, sŭb, ŭt, vĕl, and the enclitics -nĕ, -quĕ, -vĕ.

256

III. Rules for Final Syllables.

1. A final is short.

Exceptions.—Ablatives of decl. 1. mensā, bonā ; Vocative of Greek names in as, Aeneā ; and of some in es, Anchisā ; Indeclinable Numerals, trigintā ; Imperatives of conj. 1. amā (but pută) ; most Particles in a ; frustrā, intereā (but ită, quiă, short)

2. E final is short : legĕ, timetĕ, carerĕ.

> *Exceptions.*—Ablatives of declension 5. rē, diē, with the derivatives quarē, hodiē. Cases of many Greek nouns ; also famē. Adverbs formed from Adjectives ; miserē ; also ferē, fermē (but benĕ, malĕ, facilĕ, impunĕ, temĕrĕ, short). Imperatives of conj. 2. monē (but cavĕ is doubtful). Also the interjection ohē.

3. I final is long : dicī, plebī, dolī.

> *Exceptions.*—Vocatives and Datives of Greek nouns ; Chlorĭ, Thyrsidĭ ; but Datives sometimes long: Paridī. Particles ; sīcubĭ, nēcubĭ, nisĭ, quasĭ. Mihĭ, tibĭ, sibĭ, ubĭ, and ibĭ are doubtful.

4. O final is long : virgō, multō, juvō.

> *Exceptions.*—Duŏ, octŏ, egŏ, modŏ, citŏ, and a few verbs : putŏ, sciŏ. In the Silver age o was often shortened in Verbs and Nouns.

5. U final is long : cantū, dictū, diū.

6. Finals in c are long : illīc ; except nĕc and donĕc.

7. Finals in l, d, t are short : Hannibăl, illŭd, amavĭt.

8. Finals in n are short : Iliŏn, agmĕn.

> *Exceptions.*—Many Greek words : Hymēn, Ammōn.

9. Finals in r are short: calcăr, amabitŭr, Hectŏr.

> *Exceptions.*—Many Greek words : aēr, cratēr ; and compounds of pār : dispār, impār.

10. Finals in as are long : terrās, Menalcās.

> *Exceptions.*—Greek nouns of decl. 3. Arcăs (gen. -ădis), and acc. pl. lampadăs ; anăs, *a duck*.

11. Finals in ēs are long : nubēs, viderēs.

> *Exceptions.*—Cases of Greek nouns : Arcadĕs, Naiadĕs. Nominatives of a few substantives and adjectives with dental stems in ĕt, ĭt, or ĭd : segĕs, pedĕs, obsĕs ; also penĕs. Compounds of ĕs ; adĕs, potĕs.

12. Finals in is are short : dicerĭs, utilĭs, ensĭs.

> *Exceptions.*—Datives and Ablatives in īs, including gratīs, forīs. Accusatives in īs : navīs ; some Greek Nouns in īs : Salamīs. Sanguĭs, pulvĭs, doubtful. 2nd Pers. Sing. Pres. Ind. conj. 4. audīs ; compounds of vīs, sīs ; also velīs, mālīs, nolīs. In 2nd Pers. Sing. Fut. Perf. the ending is doubtful : dixerĭs.

13. Finals in os are long : ventōs, custōs, sacerdōs.

> *Exceptions.*—Greek words in ŏs (os) : Delŏs, Arcadŏs ; also compŏs, impŏs, exŏs.

14. Finals in us are short : holŭs, intŭs, amamŭs.

> *Exceptions.*—Nominatives from long stems of decl. 3. are long : virtūs, tellūs, incūs, juventūs ; the contracted cases of decl. 4. : artūs, gradūs ; and a few Greek words : Didūs, Sapphūs (genitive).

15. The Greek words chelȳs, Tiphȳs, Erinȳs have the final syllable short and the vocative ending y̆.

APPENDIX.

MEMORIAL LINES ON THE GENDER OF LATIN SUBSTANTIVES.

I. General Rules.
  The Gender of a Latin Noun
  by meaning, form, or use is shown.

1.   A Man, a name of People and a Wind,
      River and Mountain, Masculine we find:
      Rōmŭlŭs, Hispānī, Zĕphўrus, Cōcўtus, Ŏlympus.

2.   A Woman, Island, Country, Tree,
      and City, Feminine we see:
      Pēnĕlŏpē, Cўprus, Germāniă, laurŭs, Ăthēnaᴂ.

3.   To Nouns that cannot be declined
      The Neuter Gender is assigned:
      Examples fās and nĕfās give
      And the Verb-Noun Infinitive:
      Est summum nĕfās fallĕrĕ:
      Deceit is gross impiety.

Common are: săcerdōs, dux,	*priest (priestess), leader*
vātēs, părens ĕt conjux,	*seer, parent, wife (husband)*
cīvĭs, cŏmĕs, custōs, vindex,	*citizen, companion, guard, avenger*
ădŭlescens, infans, index,	*youth (maid), infant, informer*
jūdex, testĭs, artĭfex,	*judge, witness, artist*
praesŭl, exsŭl, ŏpĭfex,	*director, exile, worker*
hērēs, mīlēs, incŏlă,	*heir (heiress), soldier, inhabitant*
auctŏr, augŭr, advĕnă,	*auth.r, augur, new-comer*
hostĭs, obsĕs, praesĕs, ālĕs,	*enemy, hostage, president, bird*
pātruēlĭs ĕt sătellĕs,	*cousin, attendant*
mŭnĭceps et interprĕs,	*burgess, interpreter*
jŭvĕnĭs ĕt antistĕs,	*young person, overseer*
aurīgă, princeps: add to these	*charioteer, chief*
bōs, dammă, talpă, serpens, sūs,	*ox (cow), deer, mole, serpent, swine*
cămēlŭs, cănĭs, tīgrĭs, perdix,	
grūs.	*camel, dog, tiger, partridge, crane*

II. Special Rules for the Declensions.
Decl. 1 (A-Stems).

Rule.—Feminine in First *ă*, *ē*,
Masculine *ās*, *ēs* will be.

Exc.   Nouns denoting Males in *ă*
are by meaning Mascula:
and Masculine is found to be
Hădriă, *the Adriatic Sea.*

Decl. 2 (O-Stems).

Rule.—O-Nouns in *ŭs* and *ĕr* become
Masculine, but Neuter *um*.

Exc.   Feminine are found in *us*,
alvŭs, Arctŭs, carbăsŭs,   paunch, Great Bear, linen
cŏlŭs, hŭmŭs, pampĭnŭs,   distaff, ground, vine-leaf
vannŭs: also trees, as pĭrŭs;   winnowing-fan, pear-tree
with some jewels, as sapphĭrus;   sapphire
Neuter pĕlăgŭs and vīrŭs.   sea, poison
Vulgŭs Neuter commonly,   common people
rarely Masculine we see.

Decl. 3 (Consonant and I-Stems).

Rule 1.—Third-Nouns Masculine prefer
endings *o*, *or*, *os*, and *er*;
add to which the ending *es*,
if its Cases have increase.

Exc. (a)   Feminine exceptions show
Substantives in *dŏ* and *gŏ*.
But lĭgō, ordō, praedō, cardō,   spade, order, pirate, hinge
Masculine, and Common margō.   margin

(b)   Abstract Nouns in *ĭo* call
Fēmĭnĭnă, one and all:
Masculine will only be
things that you may touch or see,
(as curcŭliō, vespertĭlio,   weevil, bat
pŭgiō, scĭpio, and pāpĭliō)   dagger, staff, butterfly
with the Nouns that number show,
Such as ternio, sēnio.   3, 6

(c)   Ēchō Feminine we name: echo
cărō (carnis) is the same.   flesh

(*d*) Aequŏr, marmŏr, cŏr decline   *sea, marble, heart*
Neuter; arbŏr Feminine.   *tree*

(*e*) Of the Substantives in *os*,
Feminine are cōs and dōs: *whetstone, dowry*
while, of Latin Nouns, alone
Neuter are ŏs (ossĭs), *bone*,
and ōs (ōrĭs), *mouth*: a few
Greek in ŏs are Neuter too.*

(*f*) Many Neuters end in *ĕr*,
sīlĕr, ăcĕr, verbĕr, vēr,   *withy, maple, stripe, spring*
tūbĕr, ūbĕr, and cădāvĕr,   *hump, udder, carcase*
pīpĕr, ĭtĕr, and păpāvĕr.   *pepper, journey, poppy*

(*g*) Feminine are compēs, tĕgĕs,   *fetter, mat*
mercēs, mergĕs, quĭēs, sĕgĕs,   *fee, sheaf, rest, corn*
though their Cases have increase:
with the Neuters reckon aes.   *copper*

Rule 2.—Third-Nouns Feminine we class
          ending *is*, *x*, *aus*, and *as*,
          s to consonant appended,
          es in flexion unextended.

Exc. (*a*) Many Nouns in *ĭs* we find
to the Masculine assigned:
amnĭs, axĭs, caulĭs, collĭs,   *river, axle, stalk, hill*
clūnĭs, crīnĭs, fascĭs, follĭs,   *hind-leg, hair, bundle, bellows*
fustĭs, ignĭs, orbĭs, ensĭs,   *bludgeon, fire, orb, sword*
pānĭs, piscĭs, postĭs, mensĭs,   *bread, fish, post, month*
torrĭs, unguĭs, and cănālĭs,   *stake, nail, canal*
vectĭs, vermĭs, and nātālĭs,   *lever, worm, birthday*
sanguĭs, pulvĭs, cŭcŭmĭs,   *blood, dust, cucumber*
lăpĭs, cassēs, Mānēs, glīs.   *stone, nets, ghosts, dormouse*

(*b*) Chiefly Masculine we find,
sometimes Feminine declined,
callĭs, sentĭs, fūnĭs, fīnĭs,   *path, thorn, rope, end*
and in poets torquĭs, cĭnĭs.   *necklace, cinder*

(*c*) Masculine are most in *ex*
Feminine are forfex, lex,   *shears, law*
nex, sŭpellex: Common, pūmex,   *death, furniture, pumice*
imbrex, ŏbex, sĭlex, rŭmex.   *tile, bolt, flint, sorrel*

* As mĕlŏs, *melody*, ĕpŏs, *epic poem*.

(d) Add to Masculines in *ix*,
    fornix, phoenix, and cǎlix. ···· *arch, —, cup*

(e) Masculine are ădămās, ···· *adamant*
    ělěphās, mās, gǐgās, ās : ···· *elephant, male, giant, as*
    vǎs (vǎdǐs) Masculine is known, ···· *surety*
    vǎs (vāsǐs) is a Neuter Noun. ···· *vessel*

(f) Masculine are fons and mons, ···· *fountain, mountain*
    chǎlybs, hydrops, gryps, and pons, ···· *iron, dropsy, griffin, bridge*
    rǔdens, torrens, dens, and cliens, ···· *cable, torrent, tooth, client*
    fractions of the ās, as triens. ···· *four ounces*
    Add to Masculines trǐdens, ···· *trident*
    ǒriens, and ˏocǐdens, ···· *east, west*
    bǐdens (*fork*) : but bǐdens (*sheep*),
    with the Feminines we keep.

(g) Masculine are found in *ēs*
    verrēs and ăcǐnǎcēs. ···· *boar, scimetar*

Rule 3.—Third-Nouns Neuter end ǎ, ě, ar, ur, us, c, l, n, and t.

Exc. (a) Masculine are found in *ur*
    furfǔr, turtǔr, vultǔr, fūr. ···· *bran, turtle-dove, vulture, thief*

(b) Feminine in *ūs* a few
    keep, as virtūs, the long *ū* : ···· *virtue*
    servǐtūs, jŭventūs, sǎlūs, ···· *slavery, youth, safety*
    sěnectūs, tellūs, incūs, pǎlūs. ···· *old-age, earth, anvil, marsh*

(c) Also pěcǔs (pěcǔdǐs) ···· *beast*
    Feminine in Gender is.

(d) Masculine appear in *us*
    lěpǔs (lěpǒrǐs) and mūs. ···· *hare, mouse*

(e) Masculines in *l* are mūgǐl, ···· *mullet*
    consǔl, sǎl, and sōl, with pǔgǐl. ···· *consul, salt, sun, boxer*

(f) Masculine are rēn and splēn, ···· *kidney, spleen*
    pectěn, delphǐn, attǎgēn. ···· *comb, dolphin, grouse*

(g) Feminine are found in *ōn*
    Gorgōn, sindōn, halcyōn. ···· *Gorgon, cloth, king-fisher*

    Decl. 4 (U-Stems).

Rule.—Masculines end in *us*: a few are Neuter nouns, that end in *u*

Exc.   Women and trees are Feminine,
with ăcŭs, dŏmŭs, and mănŭs,   *needle, house, hand,*
trĭbŭs, Īdūs, portĭcŭs.   *tribe. the Ides, porch*

Decl. 5 (E-Stems).

Rule.—Feminine are Fifth in ēs,
Except meridiēs and diēs.   *noon, day*

Exc.   Diēs in the Singular
Common we define;
But its Plural cases are
always Masculine.

Exceptions to the Rules for the Genitive Plural of the Third Declension.

IMPARISYLLABIC NOUNS
WITH GEN. PLUR. IN **-ium.**

-ium in Plural Genitive
os (ossis) and as (assis) give;
so mas, mus, nox, and glis and lis,
with frons (frontis) and frons
(frondis);
and fons, mons, pons, and glans
and gens,
urbs too and trabs, stirps, arx and
dens,
and ars and pars, and sors and
mens.
To these add often, dos, parens,
lar, infans, serpens, and rudens;
bidens too, and aetas (aetatis)
with others ending in -as (atis).

PARISYLLABIC NOUNS
WITH GEN. PLUR. IN **-um.**

-um in Plural Genitive
pater, mater, frater give,
with accipiter and canis,
senex, sedes, juvenis;
generally too, mensis,
vates, apis, volucris.

CPSIA information can be obtained
at www.ICGtesting.com
Printed in the USA
BVOW06s2156160617

486945BV00028B/189/P